The ADHD Effect on Marriage

Understand and Rebuild Your Relationship in Six Steps

MELISSA ORLOV

Specialty Press, Inc.
3150 Willow Lane
Weston, Florida 33331
www.addwarehouse.com

Book Design and Layout: Babs Kall, Kall Graphics
2020 Update: Holly Carroll

Specialty Press, Inc.
3150 Willow Lane
Weston, Florida 33331
954-412-1332
www.addwarehouse.com

Printed in the United States of America

ISBN 978-1-886941-97-7

Library of Congress Cataloging-in-Publication Data

Orlov, Melissa.
The ADHD effect on marriage: understand and rebuild your relationship in six steps / Melissa Orlov.
p. cm.
Includes bibliographical references.
ISBN 978-1-886941-97-7
1. Attention-deficit disorder in adults. 2. Marriage—Psychological aspects. 3. Communication in marriage. 4. Married people—Psychology. I. Title.

RC394.A85O75 2010

616.85'89—dc22

2010019993

Praise for Melissa Orlov and *The ADHD Effect on Marriage*

"This book provides an incredibly valuable service to those struggling in a marriage with ADHD. Written by someone who has been there and knows firsthand how ADHD can disrupt a marriage, it will help couples truly understand ADHD, realize they are not alone, and teach them what specifically can be done to align together as a team to turn things around. Ms. Orlov has done a wonderful job of providing knowledge, awareness, and hope to those who sorely need it."

Kevin Murphy, PhD
Coauthor of *ADHD in Adults: What the Science Says*

"Melissa Orlov is one of the foremost authorities on ADHD and relationships in the world today."

Dr. Edward Hallowell
Coauthor of *Driven to Distraction and Married to Distraction*

"Millions of adults with ADHD struggle to overcome their inattention, procrastination, impulsivity, and distractibility. Yet few realize that after they marry, these same symptoms can severely affect their loved ones, often with disastrous results. Melissa Orlov offers a unique and refreshing approach to helping ADHD couples understand the underlying issues caused by ADHD that can negatively impact their relationship. Her methods are built upon years of experience and offer couples hope and guidance. Most importantly, her strategies prepare them to make smart choices to build happier, healthier futures. This book is long overdue and much needed!"

Nancy Ratey, EdM, MCC, SCAC
Author of *The Disorganized Mind: Coaching Your ADHD Brain to Take Control of Your Time, Tasks, and Talents*

The ADHD Effect is an exceptional book that addresses the complexity of the relationship between partners whose lives are affected by ADHD while presenting sound family system principles in an easy-to-understand and accessible way. Through real-life accounts in the words of adults whose marriages have been affected in this way, as well as by revealing her personal journey, Ms. Orlov provides the reader with specific ways to apply these concepts to their own partnerships. I would highly recommend this book to my clients, their partners, and to couple therapists who want to learn to effectively guide couples in marriages challenged by The ADHD Effect.

Ms. Orlov's book provides what many leave out—empathy for both partners. She offers a no-blame, nonjudgmental account of the differences and struggles of each partner, with equal amounts of respect, understanding, and empathy for the experience of both. This is a recipe for success for all partnerships.

The ADHD Effect manages to be both positive and realistic at the same time. Ms. Orlov does not underplay the challenges, but also does not pathologize or ignore the gifts and contributions each can make when ADHD is acknowledged, treated, understood, and accepted. The book balances real-life accounts that don't gloss over or minimize the difficulty of the struggle with the positive and hopeful view that through understanding, couples can come to an even closer connection. The book's basic underpinning is the idea that when individuals in a marriage stop wishing for their partners to change in ways that are not possible because of their basic biology, and instead focus on acceptance, sound strategies, and communication, their marriage can be strengthened and their differences can enliven their relationship instead of threaten it.

Sari Solden, MS, LMFT
Author of *Journeys Through ADDulthood*
(www.ADDjourneys.com)

"If you are in a marriage affected by ADHD, this book is a must read for both spouses. Save yourselves years of pain and develop the loving marriage you both deserve by reading this book and applying the information Orlov shares from her heart."

Jonathan Scott Halverstadt, LMFT
Author of *ADD & Romance*

"We adore this book! It's a comprehensive guide to dealing with the impact of ADHD on your marriage without making either partner wrong. Readers will find a wealth of information and support as well as practical tips, exercises, and stories. Our hats are off to Melissa Orlov for writing this much-needed book."

Kate Kelly and Peggy Ramundo
Coauthors of *You Mean I'm Not Lazy, Stupid or Crazy?!*
(www.adhdcoaching.com)

"Orlov's work is a beacon of light and hope, offering strategies that help couples feel happier and more satisfied."

Ari Tuckman, PsyD, MBA
Author of *More Attention, Less Deficit*

My dedication

To George, of course...
and to Kat and Alex.
You are the best!

Contents

Foreword

I will never forget meeting Melissa Orlov for the first time. She was a trustee at Phillips Exeter Academy, a prep school in New Hampshire that both of us had attended. She was doing some research at the school, and she thought I might be helpful to her. Since one of the truest loves in my life is for that school, I gladly agreed.

We met at a seafood restaurant in Cambridge called Summer Shack. Melissa arrived first. When I arrived and scanned the room, the only person I saw was someone I took to be a man because the person's hair was cut so short. This turned out to be Melissa. Her hair is much, much longer now!

She has changed in many more ways than that, as has her husband George. When I first met him, he was a short, wiry, strong-willed man who held the typical male position that he pretty much had things figured out. On the other hand, he was curious enough to learn new stuff. For example, he was willing to learn about his own ADHD. He is still a short, wiry, strong-willed man. But he has learned a lot.

Melissa and George have become—in my eyes, at least—heroes. They are heroes because they faced down dragons, fire-breathing dragons as dangerous as any Sir Gawain ever fought, and they did so with courage, grace, and honesty. They yanked their marriage from the jaws of defeat and have placed it now in a secure and joyful spot.

Having been a psychiatrist for more than three decades, I have learned what usually happens when marriages go as wrong as George's and Melissa's had gone. Usually, harsh words follow harsh deeds, betrayals surface, old wounds get ripped open, attack supplants understanding, friends take sides, the members of the couple busily justify their respective positions, blame is affixed and all but notarized, feelings sour, fond memories fade, children suffer, relatives fret, the lives of many people warp, and what once was love becomes a rancid concoction.

But Melissa and George said no to this usual way. They created a different way for themselves and their marriage. They looked at each other and asked, "Why not choose love?" And then they set about the painstaking, arduous task of rebuilding a relationship that many had written off as a lost cause.

Piece by piece, behind closed doors, they put back together an edifice that had fallen apart. Piece by piece they put back together hearts that each had broken. Piece by piece, they reassembled what each had smashed to smithereens. Day after day, week after week, month after month they did the seemingly impossible work of forgiving, understanding, connecting, and reigniting true and honest love.

One reason they are heroes in my book is that they totally defied the odds and gave me a precedent I can cite when cynics tell me that it can't be done. Many people in the field of mental health become quite cynical by the time they reach my age (sixty), and they utter wary, weary cautions against getting one's hopes up.

But Melissa and George proved that lost love can turn into a love even better than the love that was lost. This is an heroic achievement, worthy of celebration, don't you agree?

To me, this book is that celebration. And true to form, they turned their celebration into a gift for others.

Over the past five years, Melissa has been an ardent student of how ADHD influences relationships. She has studied and studied, listened and listened, and learned and learned. I daresay she is one of the foremost authorities on ADHD and relationships in the world today. Every day, from blogging to speaking to people on the phone, she offers advice based on not only her firsthand experience but also the immense knowledge she has gained through study.

She and George have had the courage to tell the world about what went wrong for them. But this book is far from a confession. It is a shrewd and smart compendium of strategies, tricks, ploys, and gambits. It is a brilliant compilation of what you can do if you are in a marriage in which one or both of you has ADHD. It is a lifesaver of a book. It is the best kind of a book, a book that can change lives for the better, and dramatically so.

Because she does not have a degree in medicine or mental health, Melissa at times wondered whether she is qualified to write this book. From her humility emerged her tenacious dedication to the task of learning everything she possibly could that might help others. As I've stated, she now is far more expert than most experts.

But she also has what few experts have. She has the benefit of her own suffering. She has the benefit of having weathered the worst kind of storm. She has the benefit of having lived what she's talking about. And she has the benefit of having prevailed.

You can trust this woman, this couple, and this book. You can learn from what's here, you can grow using what's here, and, as Melissa and George did, you can recreate love.

Edward M. Hallowell, MD

Acknowledgments

Every book has a story behind it. This one was conceived in the ashes of my "old marriage" to my wonderful husband George, who at one time wasn't so wonderful. He would be the first to admit that, but then we would both laugh and tell you that I wasn't so wonderful, either. Our marriage had broken down under the strain of undiagnosed ADHD, and changing our lives for the better felt like rolling a boulder up a mountain. As we struggled to find ways to address the issues involved with what I now call the *ADHD effect*, we realized that there just wasn't much out there about how ADHD affects marriage. So we decided to help others make the journey more quickly and, we hoped, less painfully than we did.

George is, of course, the first person I must thank here. Not only did he have the courage to give our marriage another chance, but he has also lovingly supported my dream of helping others improve their lives. He has demonstrated the depth of this support by graciously allowing me to tell even the most embarrassing parts of our story, and by managing my marriage website on a daily basis. He also has firmly taken control of his ADHD—neither of us really thinks about it much anymore. "Thank you" is inadequate, but appropriate. I love you.

Dr. Ned Hallowell also deserves thanks. He has been a mentor, friend, and teacher extraordinaire. It has been an honor and a pleasure to work with him. Thanks also to Dr. John Ratey, who introduced me to the fascinating and surprising world of the brain.

Andrea Grenadier, Julie Heflin, Cynthia Lavenson, and Babs Kall have been instrumental in getting this book "right." Talented editors, the first three pored over my manuscript and provided excellent feedback. Babs spent many long hours attending to even the smallest details of the layout. Julie gets special thanks for holding my hand on the day the bottom fell out of my marriage.

Finally, I wish to thank the thousands of contributors to my marriage blog and forum. It is your stories that have inspired me for more than a decade and have brought my book to life. For sharing your lives, feelings, and perspectives, thank you all.

A Few Notes About This Book

Technically, "ADD" no longer exists. ADHD is currently the official medical name for attention deficit disorder, with subtypes: essentially one with hyperactivity, one with distraction as the predominant feature, and one with both.*

While I will focus on common patterns in this book, ADHD does present itself differently in different people. So a statement made about "people with ADHD" or "non-ADHD spouses" is a generalization, and it should be remembered that any individual may or may not exhibit that specific characteristic. Further, some couples exhibit the issues, but in the opposite spouse. If this is the case for you, I urge you to use the information I provide and ignore the label ADHD or non-ADHD.

You will find that while I try to mix up the genders of the spouse with ADHD throughout the book—both men and women have it, after all—many examples use the masculine for the ADHD partners. This does not reflect a bias on my part. Rather, it seems that more women than men seem to be searching the Internet for relationship information and landing at my blog and forum, from which most of the examples in this book originate.

The information in this book applies not just to couples in which one spouse has ADHD, but also to couples in which both partners have ADHD. In dual-ADHD households it is often the case that one partner is better at controlling ADHD symptoms. Sometimes that partner resents the less organized spouse, thinking, "If I can make the effort to control ADHD, why can't my partner?" and some of the patterns described in this book develop. But dual-ADHD couples can also find that their intimate knowledge of ADHD helps them appreciate each other more, even if things can get chaotic.

*The psychiatric diagnostic manual is currently being updated. Part of the conversation for the next version includes whether to return to recognizing an "ADHD" with hyperactivity and an "ADD" without. In addition, there is discussion about separating adult ADHD from childhood ADHD. Whether an ADHD spouse is hyperactive does not matter for the purposes of this book.

Understanding ADHD in Your Marriage

3

The ADHD Effect

It was the best of times, it was the worst of times,
it was the age of wisdom, it was the age of foolishness,
it was the epoch of belief, it was the epoch of incredulity....
—Charles Dickens, *A Tale of Two Cities*

Marriages affected by ADHD, like all marriages, range from highly successful to completely disastrous. It is safe to say, though, that those *distorted* by ADHD symptoms sit squarely in "the worst of times." Pain and anger abound. During the worst times, you can barely talk to each other. When you do, you rarely agree or see things the same way. You're frustrated that you've gotten to this point, and you're incredulous that you haven't been able to make things better. Both of you have begun to suspect that your spouse doesn't really want to improve things. If he or she did, wouldn't things have gotten better by now?

If you are married to a person who has (or might have) ADHD, you might feel ignored and lonely in your relationship. Your spouse never seems to follow up on what he agrees to do—so much so that you may feel as if you really have another child in your home instead of an adult. You feel you're forced to remind him all the time to do things. You nag, and you've started to dislike the person you've become. The two of you either fight often or have virtually nothing to say to each other that either of you finds meaningful. You are frustrated that your spouse seems to be able to focus intently on things that interest him, but never on you. Perhaps worst of all, you feel intense stress from not knowing whether you can rely on him and feeling saddled with almost all of the responsibilities of the household, while your spouse gets to "have all the fun."

If you have ADHD, (or think you do), you may feel as if the person you married is buried deep within a nagging monster that lives in your home. The person you had cherished has been transformed into a control freak, trying to manage every single detail of your life together. No matter how hard you try, you can never do well enough for your spouse, even if you are successful elsewhere, such as in your work. The easiest way to deal with her is simply to leave her alone. You're willing to admit that you make mistakes sometimes, but so does she—and certainly, no one is perfect. You wish she would just relax once in a while and live life as a happy person, instead of a harpy.

If either of these descriptions sounds familiar, you are suffering from what I call the *ADHD effect*. Your courtship was happy and exciting (and often fast), but your marriage has been completely different. You may feel desperately unhappy and lonely, and your partner isn't even aware of it—even if you've tried to talk about it. You fight and nag much more than you expected, and life often seems depressingly up and down and out of control. The underlying reason could be that ADHD symptoms--and the responses both of you have to those symptoms—have been destroying your partnership.

The good news is that understanding the role that ADHD plays can turn your marriage around. In *The ADHD Effect on Marriage*, you will learn how to identify ADHD and the issues it brings to marriages, as well as specific steps you can take to begin to rebuild your lives.

You will be surprised by the consistency and predictability of the patterns in marriages affected by ADHD. These patterns start with an ADHD symptom that triggers a series of predictable responses in both spouses, creating a downward spiral in your marriage. In this case, knowledge is power. You both contribute to these patterns. If you know what they are, you can also change them or avoid them altogether.

This book is the guide my husband and I wish we had from the beginning. It will take you through the steps needed to regain your footing in your relationship, repair the emotional damage, and create a path into a brighter and more satisfying future. You'll find out that your problems aren't because of character flaws or failings, but are the result of the *ADHD effect*—and that the two of you together can overcome it. You'll learn how to put ADHD back where it belongs: as just one of many aspects of your lives, not as the overwhelming determinant of your days.

The Stakes Are High: The Research on Divorce and ADHD

The stakes are high. Research on how ADHD affects marriage suggests that many of these marriages founder under the misunderstandings and issues that ADHD symptoms add to the relationship. It is quite possible that you are currently considering divorce, or have done so at some point in your marriage. If so, you would not be alone.

According to one study, a person who has ADHD is almost twice as likely as one who does not have ADHD to be divorced. A different study suggests that 58 percent of relationships with at least one person with ADHD are clinically dysfunctional—twice that of the non-ADHD population.[1] These frightening statistics reinforce just how difficult many of these relationships become. However, these statistics do not mean that people with ADHD can't make good spouses. In these marriages, both partners fall victim to a combination of ADHD symptoms and their mutual responses (and lack of responses) to those symptoms.

1. The first notable study on divorce and separation rates for adults with ADHD was done by Biederman et al. in 1993, and was replicated by Murphy and Barkley in 1996. Both of these studies used older participants than later studies done by Barkley et al, which showed less elevated divorce rates but very elevated dysfunction rates (58% of marriages). Given that marital dissatisfaction builds over time with the repetitive introduction of ADHD symptoms into relationships, I find that these studies are consistent with what I observe: that things can be bad right away, with dysfunctional patterns between spouses building, eventually leading to divorce if not addressed. For more details about all of these studies, see *ADHD in Adults: What the Science Says* by Russell A. Barkley, Kevin R. Murphy and Mariellen Fischer, The Guilford Press, 2008, pp. 380-384.

I see evidence of this every day. Thousands of couples have shared their ADHD marital stories at www.adhdmarriage.com, the blog and forum I have run with Dr. Edward Hallowell since 2007. The challenges these couples face are significant, as well as often shockingly familiar. They share their deepest feelings, experiences, and dreams.

Untreated or incompletely treated ADHD can be *really* hard to live with for both partners. Symptoms create real physical, financial, and mental hardship. But there is something else going on, too. What I have observed at the blog, in my seminar, and in my consulting practice with couples, is that a great deal of damage is caused by lack of knowledge about, and misinterpretation of, ADHD symptoms. Couples who learn about the specific patterns that emerge in these relationships can learn how to avoid them. That's why this book addresses all of the following:

- Identifying and interpreting ADHD symptoms in adults
- Why treating ADHD effectively is critical, and what "effective treatment" looks like within a relationship
- Finding ways to interact that are positive for both of you while taking the presence of ADHD into account

The Rewards of Rebuilding Your ADHD-Affected Marriage

A brief overview of my own story will demonstrate that even the most dysfunctional marriages can improve and thrive with the right knowledge, understanding, compassion, emotional strength, and a determination to move past marital history.

Like many couples, my husband and I had no idea that one of us had ADHD. I had fallen in love with my husband's brilliance, sharp wit, and penchant for adventure. He is a lover of music, food, and wine, and he breathed unexpected excitement into my life with love, attention, gifts, and surprise trips. He focused on me with a ferocity that both surprised and flattered me. He was accomplished and professionally successful, yet warm; when I got sick on our first date,

I was touched that he tucked me under a blanket on the sofa and made me hot tea.

But in its early years, our marriage began to fall apart, despite the fact that we loved each other. I couldn't understand how someone who had started out so attentive could now ignore me and my needs so completely, or be so "consistently inconsistent" when it came to carrying his weight around the house and with the children. He sometimes helped out, but usually didn't, and often seemed to be unaware of my existence. As it turned out, he was equally confused and annoyed. How could the woman he had married, who had seemed so warm and optimistic, change into an exhausted nag who wouldn't give him a break and wouldn't leave him alone?

By our ten-year anniversary, we were completely dysfunctional as a couple and contemplating divorce. We were held together only by our desire to raise our children well and a feeling deep inside that we ought to be able to do better. We were angry, frustrated, completely disconnected, and deeply unhappy. I was clinically depressed. Around that time, our daughter, at age nine, was diagnosed with both a math learning disability and ADHD.

We did not know that ADHD is extremely heritable—comparable in its heritability to height.[2] If you have a child with ADHD, chances are good that one of the biological parents has ADHD. Eventually, we learned of this connection and confirmed through a full evaluation that my husband has ADHD. This started a battle over whether he should treat it, and how he—and I—should respond. This kind of battle is typical. For some people the diagnosis is a relief and a new beginning; for others, like my husband, it seems a threat to their status, self-knowledge, and self-image. How much should one change? For whom is one changing? Over time, and with the right kinds of support, most with ADHD can accept the implications of their diagnosis and make their lives, and the lives of their partners, better.

2. About half of children whose parents have ADHD also have ADHD. Research done by Biederman et al. in 1995 put the chances of an adult with diagnosed ADHD having a child with ADHD at 57 percent, while in 2003 Minde et al. placed it lower, at 43 percent. For more detail about these studies and the heritability of ADHD, as well as the heritability of coexisting conditions, see *ADHD in Adults: What the Science* Says by Russell A. Barkley, Kevin R. Murphy, and Mariellen Fischer, The Guilford Press, 2008, pp. 384-393.

Discovering that one or both of you has ADHD is just the beginning. Medication is the most efficient way to jump-start treatment, but it does not effectively treat ADHD in marriages without the addition of behavioral changes. *These changes must be voluntary.* No matter how much a non-ADHD spouse may want to, she can't "make" her spouse do certain things like be more organized or more attentive. Furthermore, *these changes must come from both partners.* Changes only in the ADHD spouse don't resolve the marriage's issues. We learned both ideas the hard way, mostly at my husband's expense, as I kept trying to force him to do things differently. The harder I pushed, the more he resisted, and the worse our relationship became. Sound familiar?

I am asking you to come on a journey of change, not offering a quick fix. (If I did offer that, would you believe that I can deliver it?) The rewards of the journey are worth it. My husband and I have moved from completely dysfunctional to almost ridiculously happy. We are thriving as individuals and feel that our relationship is stronger now than it has ever been. Back "in love," we feel safer and more optimistic than on the day we married. My husband's ADHD symptoms are under control, and I have a much stronger understanding and appreciation of the effort that takes. Unlike during our difficult times, we know and accept each other's faults and rejoice in each other's strengths. Our pride in our ability to pull ourselves back from the brink helps us to celebrate our feelings in ways that are loving and supportive. Though our marriage can have bumps, we are now resilient and have the tools to recover with good speed. We won't ever go back to our difficult past, and have crafted a new relationship and brilliant future.

You can do this, too. You can move past your current unhappiness and create something better than you could have ever dreamed possible.

ADHD and Its Diagnosis

"I have seen too many people with ADD prevail over their problems to ever believe it's impossible. Everyone who has ADD can sculpt a fulfilling, joyful life out of what they've been born with....Doing so starts in your head and in your heart: you need knowledge and you need hope."

— Dr. Edward Hallowell

At the extremes of opinion, ADHD is either a terrible "disorder" that can ruin your life or a "way of being in the world" that is misunderstood by many and can be considered a gift when properly treated. Both views are supported by the same research; they simply represent different approaches to thinking about and treating ADHD.

The "curse" camp points to the statistics—historically, people with ADHD have fared worse than those without ADHD in many life functions (holding jobs, staying happily married, staying out of jail). This is "proof" that ADHD is a problem that needs to be treated as a dysfunction or an illness, much in the same way one would treat a physical illness or a disease.

The "gift" camp believes that people with ADHD have many wonderful attributes that can be obscured by their symptoms. This group believes in the power of human inspiration and willpower to change one's circumstances. They know that it takes a lot of hard work to change the habits developed in response to ADHD symptoms so that one can thrive in the world. Change, they say, can best come from hope and inspiration.

After years of dealing with both child and adult ADHD in my own family, as well as advising couples struggling with ADHD, I take a modified positive approach. Being realistic about the great stress ADHD can place on both spouses is critical to dealing with ADHD in your relationship. Yet optimism is also critically important. I have seen firsthand the benefits that being positive can provide. My daughter, a smart, creative, lovely woman of nineteen at the time this book was first written, has her share of challenges created by her ADHD symptoms. Yet I heard her tell a friend, "I wouldn't want to be without ADHD. It's the reason I am who I am—creative, able to think differently, able to see the world in fresh ways." She recognizes that every individual is unique, and she attributes much of her specialness—for better and for worse—to her ADHD "way of being." Now 28, she has a masters degree in UX research with which she can utilize the power of her endless, ADHD-inspired, curiosity.

When the harder aspects of ADHD symptoms are accepted as the flip side of the very positive aspects of ADHD, a balance can be achieved that is similar to the balance that people without ADHD create for themselves. I, for example, do not have ADHD, but I do have specific weaknesses that I acknowledge and work around in my everyday life. I generally have not needed medication to help me achieve that balance, though I found that the experience of treating depression with medication for several years (and the dramatic improvement in my outlook that this medication provided) helped me to gain greater respect for the benefits and limits of psychotropic medications. My daughter, with the help of ADHD medications in low doses, has found her own balance point. Like me, she has strengths she pursues with passion, and weaknesses she must accommodate. But I am confident that if her father and I had treated her as if she had a terrible disorder, she would have matured with quite a different opinion of herself and likely had different results from her efforts.

What Is ADHD?

Technically, ADHD is a series of symptoms that can be identified by a medical professional with training in ADHD evaluation through specific tests and the compilation of a medical history. The heritability of the condition, along with MRI research studies, suggest that there is a biological underpinning for ADHD in the brain. Dr. John Ratey, an expert on how the brain functions, suggests that ADHD is the result of dysregulation of the reward system (primarily dopamine) in the brain. In short, the brain of a person with ADHD does not move dopamine and other chemicals in the attention areas of the brain in the same way that the brain of someone without ADHD does. This chemical difference results in the symptoms associated with ADHD. Social pressures at home, at work, and at school often exacerbate a person's response to ADHD, and can create additional conditions such as anxiety or depression.

The diagnostic criteria for ADHD include comparing a patient to a series of statements, taking a detailed patient history, and, rarely, administering brain wave tests (qEEG) or SPECT scans. These last two are not necessary (or even recommended) for diagnosis, but can be helpful in very limited circumstances. A patient history is always needed for diagnosis, as this is critical for differentiating ADHD from other syndromes that share some of its symptoms. Only a well-trained professional can tell the difference between bipolar disorder and ADHD, for example, or can discern whether you have coexisting conditions such as learning disabilities, anxiety, depression, or oppositional defiance disorder (ODD).

Drs. Russell Barkley, Kevin Murphy, and Mariellen Fischer have studied how to appropriately translate the current child-centered criteria for diagnosing ADHD to adults.[3] They have concluded that four criteria can diagnose the *inattentive* side of adult ADHD with 95 percent accuracy or better. These criteria are as follows:

- Fails to pay close attention to details
- Has difficulty organizing tasks
- Loses things necessary for tasks
- Is easily distracted

Of these symptoms, chronic distraction is the one that is most important for a diagnosis of ADHD.

3. *ADHD in Adults: What the Science Says* by Russell A. Barkley, Kevin R. Murphy, and Mariellen Fischer, The Guilford Press, 2008, pp. 113-116.

On the *hyperactivity* side of ADHD, they suggest that adult patients can be diagnosed accurately about 90 percent of the time with these criteria:

- Feels restless
- Has difficulty engaging in leisure quietly
- Talks excessively
- Has difficulty awaiting turn

Dr. Hallowell expands on the panel research data used by Barkley et al. and the diagnostic manual to paint a broader picture of symptoms based on his clinical work. He looks for the following:

- A sense of underachievement and insecurity (regardless of how much one has actually accomplished)
- Difficulty getting organized
- Chronic procrastination or trouble getting started
- Many projects going on simultaneously, trouble with follow-through
- Easily distracted, tendency to drift off
- An intolerance of boredom
- Impatience, low tolerance of frustration
- Impulsivity, verbally or in action; often with reference to money
- Mood swings
- Physical or cognitive restlessness
- Tendency toward addictive behavior
- Frequent search for high stimulation, tendency to be a maverick
- Inaccurate self-observation[4]

If you are having problems in your marriage, many of them are likely related directly to the issues surrounding these ADHD symptoms. On the plus side, however, people with ADHD can also be creative, original thinkers. Many are quick to forgive, warm, and easygoing. Chances are that some of these positive ADHD traits are the reason you fell in love with your ADHD partner in the first place!

ADHD as a Reward-Deficiency Syndrome

Dr. John Ratey, a leading expert in both ADHD and the brain, suggests that ADHD can be thought of as a *reward-deficiency syndrome* created from a deficit of specific pleasure neurotransmitters (most importantly dopamine, but also serotonin and endorphins) that are used to indicate reward in the attention centers of the brain. He notes that without these chemical indicators of reward, people with ADHD have trouble completing tasks that reward only after a long period, such as doing well in college to obtain a better job. A lack of dopamine may explain the drug addiction and thrill-seeking behavior of some with ADHD. These activities stimulate the production of dopamine. In any event, without sufficient levels of these neurotransmitters, an ADHD spouse's attention is inconsistent and becomes dysregulated.

> These insights explain why dopaminergic medications like Ritalin, Dexedrine, and Cylert are used to treat ADHD. They work by both exciting presynaptic dopamine receptors and inhibiting molecules that clear synapses of dopamine. The antidepressant Wellbutrin, also used to treat ADHD, similarly increases dopamine levels in the brain.[5]

4. A useful overview of ADHD and its diagnosis can be found at Dr. Hallowell's website, under ADD/ADHD overview, at www.drhallowell.com. This includes the diagnostic manual information, as well as Hallowell's expanded list of statements that can help you determine whether to seek an evaluation.

5. Ratey, John J., *A User's Guide to the Brain: Perception, Attention, and the Four Theaters of the Brain*, Vintage Books, 2002, pp. 127-128.

That reward-focused, or reward-seeking brain can easily engage with a favorite sport, interesting friends, social media, and anything else that stimulates it. Sadly, that same brain has very real difficulty staying engaged with repetitive household tasks, planning for the future, doing taxes and anything else that is boring, repetitive, or overwhelming. This is true even if there is a 'reward' in the future, such as saving now (boring!) to be able to have money for retirement (that's in the 'not now').

What does this mean to you and your spouse? It means that ADHD is real. The symptoms you experience are the result of how the ADHD brain produces, and then regulates, specific chemicals in your brain. Think of the degree to which the more familiar chemicals estrogen and progesterone can affect a woman's body, attitude, and spirit, and you may well agree that chemicals can make a big difference—and so can regulating them.

I am frequently asked whether the fact that ADHD involves a chemical imbalance means an adult with ADHD must take medication. Whether to take medication is a personal choice, and there are other ways to treat ADHD, although they often require the kind of "stick-to-it-iveness" that people with untreated ADHD have trouble managing. Further, research suggests medications are some of the most effective treatments for ADHD. So at least *trying* ADHD medications to see if they work for you as one part of a treatment plan seems to be a good approach. Many of these medications have been available for a long time and their side effects are well known. In addition, those in the stimulant category are very short acting, so even if you try one and hate it, you are stuck with it for only a few hours before it is out of your system. (The exception here being an allergic reaction or heart problem, both of which are very rare.) With experimentation to get the dosing right, more than 70 percent of patients in Dr. Ned Hallowell's clinics report that medication helps them, without negative side effects. Dr. Hallowell also points out that there are specific side effects of *not* treating ADHD, such as low self-esteem, chronic job problems, and, in many cases, marital problems.

All medications, of course, should be tried under the direction and observation of your doctor, whom you should make familiar with your medical history. Be sure to discuss how ADHD medications might interact with other medications you may be taking or whether you might have heart problems.

Coexisting Conditions in the ADHD Spouse

Dr. Russell Barkley and his colleagues posit that more than 80 percent of adults with ADHD have at least one other condition, more than 50 percent have two or more, and more than one-third have three or more other conditions[6] (Note that these numbers are not for children diagnosed with ADHD, as some of these disorders develop with age. Also note that the numbers come from many different research studies, hence ranges are presented.) These include the following:

- Current depression: 16 to 31 percent
- Depression at some point in lifetime: 53 percent
- Anxiety: 24 to 43 percent, depending on a variety of factors
- Oppositional defiant disorder: 24 to 35 percent
- Conduct disorder: 17 to 25 percent (rates can be higher if diagnosed as hyperactive when a child)
- Alcohol dependence or abuse at some point in lifetime: 21 to 53 percent

These statistics are not meant to scare you. Rather, they suggest that ADHD is not benign, needs immediate attention, and requires some very specific approaches.

6. For a detailed overview of coexisting psychiatric issues, including ODD, CD, depression, and anxiety, see *ADHD in Adults: What the Science Says* by Russell A. Barkley, Kevin R. Murphy, and Mariellen Fischer, The Guilford Press, 2008, pp. 205-244. The specific numbers quoted in my text come from pages 205-206, 223, 241.

Tips
Getting a Good Diagnosis

- **A good diagnosis of *all* potential disorders is best.** Take the time to get a full evaluation, not just a superficial "Sounds as if you have ADHD, why don't you try some meds?"
- **You are not qualified to accurately "diagnose" your spouse,** even if you think you see symptoms of ADHD. Things that "look like ADHD" to an untrained eye might be something else, or ADHD might be present along with other issues that also should be addressed. Remember that 80 percent of adults with ADHD have an additional mental health issue at one time or another.
- **Make sure to treat *all* of the disorders present.** This may well require multiple medications as well as therapy for anxiety or depression. Treating only the ADHD, or only another disorder when ADHD is present, can be far less effective than treating the entire spectrum. As an example, ADHD is often a factor in an adult's depression or anxiety. Treating the depression without treating the ADHD means that you are not treating the underlying disorder. On the other hand, depression can get in the way of treating ADHD. If you can't drag yourself out of bed in the morning, you are unlikely to make the behavioral changes needed to address ADHD.
- **Due to the nature of ADHD, treating it is a matter of doctor-supervised experimentation.** Don't give up if one medication or dosage doesn't work. Try other types of medications or other dosages until a balance is achieved that provides optimal symptom relief and no meaningful side effects. Another option is to try genetic testing to help narrow choices about which meds might work for you.
- **Try to take a big-picture view of the issues that you face as a couple.** Learning about ADHD may help you identify ADHD-specific behaviors, but learning about depression, if that is diagnosed, will also help.

If you have ADHD now, you had it as a child, even if it wasn't diagnosed. Typical indicators that ADHD might have been present in childhood include teacher's reports that mention "unfulfilled potential" and fidgety or forgetful behavior; academic and social struggles, particularly in high school and college; and being labeled a "space cadet" by friends. Recognize, however, that some people with ADHD compensated for their ADHD in childhood but fall apart after they have too much on their plate as adults. Typically, this happens with the introduction of children into your lives. Raising kids takes an inordinate amount of organizational skill, which is not generally an ADHD strong point.

Symptoms in the Non-ADHD Spouse

ADHD spouses are not the only ones who can have symptoms that need treatment. Living with an ADHD spouse can be tremendously stressful for a non-ADHD spouse if a couple does not have good coping strategies in place. Disappointment and fear can lead to depression and anxiety, and stress responses can lead to many physical symptoms. The non-ADHD spouse's symptoms should be treated by a doctor and addressed through better stress management, such as regular exercise, plenty of sleep, good nutrition, meditation, and other methods. Non-ADHD spouses need to focus on their health with at least as much intensity as they focus on their partner's condition in order to remain healthy.

Ways of Being, or You are Not Like Me!

It is important to realize that ADHD is not always a "disorder," in spite of its name. It can be thought of as a collection of traits and tendencies that define a way of being in the world. It is only when the negative traits associated with ADHD become disabling that ADHD requires treatment. Conversely, when treated properly, a person formerly disabled by ADHD symptoms can often control their ADHD so that it once again becomes simply a way of being in the world.

How both of you think about ADHD is actually very important. Having a "disorder" can suggest an illness that is perceived as "bad" and permanent. Thinking of ADHD as a series of traits that can be both positive and negative, and that can be managed with the right strategies, is far more likely to encourage optimism, effort, and patience.

It is the trap of the non-ADHD spouse to feel that he or she is "normal" and the ADHD spouse is "not normal." This usually unspoken sense of superiority, or assumption that the non-ADHD partner's way of doing things is more "reasonable" than the ADHD partner's approach, dooms many relationships. Consider the words of this fiancée:

> Recently my husband-to-be has [started talking] about his ADHD. I embraced his feelings of realization that he had a problem, and I dug into it and talked about it for days with him in hopes that seeking professional help would help us out. The last few months have been rough, especially before marriage!
>
> I do not want my hubby to feel like I know he's broken, I want him to feel whole even though we both know he's broken. It would probably be best if he feels like I still think of him as a whole, and I'll support him no matter even if he goes through therapy for his ADHD.

This woman's point of view is truly a recipe for disaster, but it is distressingly common. Imagine being married to someone who thinks you are "broken," but figures you won't understand she feels that way if she is nice enough to you or accommodates you well enough. What do you think the chances are that this man doesn't already know her feelings after several days of "talks" about his "problem"?

People with ADHD are all too aware that others think they are "broken," and the resulting low self-esteem and resentment sometimes color their ability to enter into a relationship in the first place. Take this professionally successful woman with ADHD:

> To all the non-ADD spouses reading this: thanks for loving your ADD spouses, from a single woman who wishes she had a spouse, ADD or non-ADD, who could understand.

> Despite a master's degree in social work, medication, weekly therapy, supportive friends and family, and a very introspective, analytical mind that is hyper-focused on my behaviors and impact on others, ADD still plagues me.
>
> And I'm afraid, really afraid, to show someone the ADD completely. Because I actually am not quite sure that I can get it all in control "enough" for someone.

On the flip side, some with ADHD have difficulty understanding the less spontaneous lives of those without ADHD. You might hear "Can't you just relax a bit and take things as they come?" from the ADHD partner, who is used to adapting as life changes.

You and your spouse are two different people. But do you understand how those differences are expressed? Let's consider some of the differences between how people with and without ADHD perceive and inhabit the world. If I paint an accurate picture, I hope you'll see how your differences can enliven your relationship, and that you'll start to cultivate an empathy that will help you move past your current issues.

The Energy and Speed of ADHD

Dr. Ned Hallowell compares living with ADHD to driving in the rain with bad windshield wipers at about 90 miles per hour. Every once in a while, things are very clear, but most of the time you're not completely sure what's coming at you—and it's coming fast! Dr. Hallowell is referring to two kinds of speed here: the bracing, euphoric, exciting variety (think race-car driving) as well as the speed and all-encompassing way that information comes at a person with ADHD. The ADHD brain has few filters on it; often, everything enters at once, and in a big jumble. This provides some interesting dilemmas in a world that values hierarchy, but it is also an opportunity.

Embracing speed is one aspect of ADHD with which many non-ADHD spouses struggle. While it may have been exciting during your courtship, it seems more threatening, and sometimes exhausting, once you've settled into a marriage. I thought it was cool when my husband showed up for our first date in a Porsche 911. It didn't matter that Porsches are terrible in the snow, or that we had to put our skis through the sunroof in order to drive out of town. (Brrrr!!!) Wow! It was exciting! But after we got married his fast driving turned into a negative. He drove too quickly for my comfort, and for many years, though he disagreed, I worried that his aggressive driving might endanger our kids.

It's not just fast driving. It's also a speed of living life that can be a mismatch within a relationship. Listen to the words of this exhausted spouse:

> My husband of seventeen years was diagnosed with ADHD a few years ago and he felt a revelation inside, an "a-ha!" moment, if you will. He finally had pin-pointed what he had been feeling since childhood. Placed in a resource room in school because of his grades, but always winning the heart of his teachers with his wit, sense of humor and energy, he managed to get through high school. Receiving a soccer scholarship for college was the first real test to see if he could function on his own, only to fail out after two years because he couldn't manage "it all." No wonder?
>
> He took risks as an adult, married with three kids, and successfully owns his own business. He is a motivational speaker and "Wows" his participants with his energy, creativity and enthusiasm…call it passion. So what is wrong? Sounds all good, right?
>
> Then why do I feel like he is a roommate, instead of a life-partner? He travels a lot and the dynamic of our marriage is this. He leaves and everything is in order (and believe me I am not a "stick in the mud," I do give in and I have become very flexible over the years and with three boys). I was home with my kids when they

> were young (basically raising them alone), and now I am back teaching elementary school and working full time. When he travels, life is a routine, and just the way I like it. Then all "hell" breaks loose when he arrives home. He is like a whirlwind. I just have such a hard time transitioning and he is off in his own world when he is home....

To this woman, a "comfortable" life is one that includes a predictable routine and quiet, intimate, shared time with her husband. I suspect that this is at least in part because routine makes taking care of three boys much easier. Her husband's energy level is disruptive and foreign. Yet this is inherently part of him; the energy, humor, and wit that have gotten him out of tough spots in the past are the key to his professional success and are likely a reason why his wife was initially attracted to him (before she needed the routine to help make her and the children's lives easier). Neither spousal style is wrong in this situation; her routine helps her succeed as a mother, and his energy helps him succeed at work. It is the intersection of their styles at this particular time in their lives that creates the problems.

Chances are that this couple can improve their relationship if they are both willing to make concessions. With treatment for his ADHD, it is quite possible he could retain his energy but focus it more effectively so that it isn't so disruptive to her routine. He could empathize with her need for routine and join her in some family activities that demonstrate his respect for her. Once his energy wasn't so disruptive, she would feel less threatened by it, and might be able to schedule appropriate times to drop her routines and jump into his whirlwind for the sake of strengthening their bond, as she likely did during their courtship. Each would remain essentially the same person, but their intersection could invigorate their lives with variety, companionship, respect, and support.

Impulse Control

Living with ADHD is somewhat like having a race-car brain that lacks good brakes. Impulse control is a huge issue; people with ADHD often have minds that go fast and have trouble stopping when they need to. Have you ever noticed how hard it is for the ADHD spouse to *stop* doing a project she likes (watching television or working on the computer, for example)? Or that she'll blurt out an idea or thought before thinking it through?

Ask a person with ADHD why he brings home a pound of chocolate but only half of what was on the grocery list, or why he just spent $100 on gifts when he knew you needed the money to pay the electric bill, and he might say, "I don't know." This would be an accurate description of the impulsivity of the moment. But now, in fact, you *do* know. People with untreated ADHD have really bad brakes.

It is difficult for someone who doesn't have ADHD to understand this lack of impulse control. People without ADHD expect that adults have learned how to control their impulses in their own and others' best interests, yet are faced over and over again with the fact that this is not the case for their spouses. ADHD partners can blurt out hurtful comments, ruin family finances, start affairs on a whim, or give in to road rage because their untreated brains don't have brakes. All of it is emotionally painful for the non-ADHD spouse, and often for the ADHD spouse as well.

Not *meaning* to hurt someone, however, isn't enough. Overwhelming debt, the emotional sting of "too much honesty," or an affair can all tear relationships apart. It is important that the ADHD spouse consider impulsiveness a symptom that needs treatment, not just part of a happy-go-lucky personality.

Now and Not Now

The joke is that there are really only two time zones for a person with ADHD: "now" and "not now"! A person with ADHD is very present focused. Often, something that was going on ten minutes earlier is out of mind, as is the thing that is supposed to happen ten minutes in the future.

This "present-ness" shows up in a number of ways in marriage. Your ADHD wife, for example, may have trouble remembering what you talked about not too long ago. She may know that it's good to save money for the future, yet have trouble staying focused on that goal when spending right now seems so much more appealing. It may seem as if you have the same arguments over and over again…and you probably do, in part because that last one you had was in the "not now." Another explanation is that people with ADHD often have bad short-term memories, so they might not remember having had the argument earlier. Creating physical ways to remember, such as lists or taking notes, can help bring previous conversations back into the "now" when needed.

Another way to think of now and not now is to imagine you have "time tunnel vision." Here is how one man with ADHD describes how he interacts with time:

> I often use this analogy: I look at time through a paper towel roll moving from left to right on a timeline. I see only what is in my vision at that moment. As I progress along the timeline, the thoughts and sights that were in my little window have passed to the left and are often forgotten. If I act on things in the window I can be somewhat successful. If I miss it, it could be gone forever. I also cannot see or think about the time to the right of my window. This makes it difficult to plan ahead. (For instance, I have a hard time planning for the weekend and before you know it, the weekend is here and I have no plans.)

Being aware of now and not now (or time tunnel vision, if you prefer that) can work in your favor. For example, you're aware that staying focused on boring tasks can be hard for those with ADHD. While this has to do with distractibility and reward-deficiency issues, the solution can be found in the now and not now mentality. If you can create an emotionally neutral yet effective system of reminders that brings a forgotten task back into the now *at the right time,* you have a much better chance of getting it done. I say "emotionally neutral" because it is important to choose a way that doesn't make the ADHD person defensive. "Effective" is whatever works for that particular person. Setting an alarm or putting a note in a lunch box to remember a noon phone call can be neutral and effective. Nagging and berating is never so.

Emotional Hyper-Arousal

Many people with ADHD have trouble regulating their emotions, particularly on the negative side. They are easily triggered into irritability or anger, even around things that seem minor to others.

There are a number of reasons for this. On the physiological side of things, researchers at the University of Pennsylvania note that the ADHD brain creates overly abundant emotional responses, while the impulse control systems (or "brakes") to manage those responses are poor. Where others may feel anger but keep a lid on those feelings, those with ADHD just let it out. Both issues – too much emotion and weak brakes – have to do with the neurochemistry of the brain.[6b]

> We have a joke in our family – when my husband gets upset really quickly he might say 'I just lost my brakes!' This lessens the tension and helps us both settle back down.

On the emotional side of things, adults with ADHD have often spent their lives being critiqued by others. Even if it's well meant, a "you could do so much better if you would only try harder" from a teacher, parent or friend really stings if you know how hard you are already working to manage distraction, organization, planning and impulsivity. Over the course of many years, regular comments on ADHD under-performance lead to a hyper-sensitivity to criticism.

This sensitivity is often baffling to non-ADHD partners who don't

6b. CHADD International Conference on ADHD, 2019 Keynote address by Anthony Rostain, MD, MA

have the same brain chemistry or history. They say something that they think is pretty neutral or that they themselves would take in stride. To be fair, their comments may be about something an ADHD partner didn't do, so could easily be considered a critique. Nonetheless, because the non-ADHD partner would not be fazed by a similar comment, they can be quite surprised at the intensity of their ADHD partner's response.

Frustrations also rise quickly and spread broadly when you have ADHD. One time when I was talking with my husband by phone while he was walking to his hotel room, our conversation went from happy to irritable and mean in very short order. What had happened? His room entry key had malfunctioned. But with poor brakes, his immediate irritation and frustration with the key came shooting directly at me and felt like an attack. In a similar vein, I have learned to avoid interacting with him when he is packing for a business trip, which he usually does last minute and is stressed about. His irritability in these times simply doesn't make it worth it to me to get in his line of fire.

The issue with ADHD emotional hyper-arousal is that it is destabilizing for relationships. If negative emotional responses are unpredictable, that leaves the other partner walking on eggshells – unsure when they will suddenly be under fire. It feels treacherous and unsafe, making it difficult for the non-ADHD partner to relax into the relationship or feel affectionate. If you are an ADHD partner with emotional hyper-arousal, please do everything you can to better manage your emotional outbursts, irritability and anger. Don't wait to do this, even if there are other things in your relationship, such as anger your spouse expresses towards you, that make you wonder about the importance of your own emotional responses. If you have a fast trigger you will *always* benefit from learning how to manage it better…and not just at home. Your work relationships will improve, too.

My husband and I now know that frustration spill over, quick responses, easy anger, and emotional hyper-arousal are part of ADHD. In response, we have created work arounds to move us away from poor interactions resulting from emotional hyper-arousal. These include:

- **Setting emotional impulsivity as a target symptom** for the ADHD partner. Medication, exercise and mindfulness can all help the ADHD partner improve his or her emotional brakes.
- **Avoiding discussing difficult topics during 'high irritability' times of day**, such as before the ADHD partner has had coffee or when s/he is exhausted. As an extension, avoiding the ADHD partner when high stress activities (like packing when late) almost always leads to extreme irritability.
- **Creating redirection verbal cues** when irritability spills over towards the other partner. Ours is a polite but firm "I understand you're frustrated by X, but please don't point it in my direction." My husband will immediately apologize and calm himself down.
- **Having the non-ADHD partner be aware of the fast trigger topics** for the ADHD partner and make sure to approach him or her in a 'soft' way rather than just starting right in on a difficult topic. This helps the partner settle more gently into a topic and discourages "brake failure."

Planning

Though not true in all cases, people with ADHD often have trouble planning ahead. Planning means *organizing* a number of different options into a workable game plan and *anticipating* what will happen in various scenarios. Executive function differences in the ADHD brain often don't accommodate these common skills. One upside of not being natural planners is that people with ADHD can be really good at going with the flow, making things work in real time.

It's not unusual for a person with ADHD to be attracted to a partner who is a good planner. In courtship, his ability to organize and plan helps to make things happen, and her easy going nature provides liveliness and spontaneity. They both benefit and thrive. After kids, though, the ADHD partner's inability to plan becomes a real negative as the organizational demands imposed by taking care of children require that both pitch in to keep life from becoming overwhelming.

People with ADHD can put coping strategies in place that help them to plan more effectively, but both members of the couple need to be conscious that this requires significant effort and lots of organizational tools such as lists, charts, conversations, and the like. Don't assume that just because you are both adults, you can also both plan well.

Other Perspectives on Time

One of the major differences between how people with and without ADHD lead their lives has to do with how they experience time. This is more than just a symptom or two. People with ADHD are notoriously late because they can lose track of time, and they are often terrible judges of how long it will take them to complete a task.

The people I know with ADHD simply *relate* to time differently than I do. I can use my past experiences to predict quite closely how long it will take me to do something familiar. This is often not the case for people with ADHD. Their relationship with time is much more fluid: fast and slow, like a roller coaster.

Distraction sometimes distorts time. My daughter's curiosity often leads her to become intrigued by specific subtasks of what she is doing (following an interesting idea longer than necessary when researching a paper, for example). Sometimes she follows one interesting thread, sometimes thirteen. This helps her learn all sorts of interesting details, but can result in missing a deadline. Since she doesn't know ahead of time how intriguing things will be, she is unpredictable in how she uses her time. She has learned to set mini-goals to keep herself on track and to budget lots more time to do things than her non-ADHD peers might require.

My husband is in another camp. He could be called a "time optimist." While he's fairly consistent with how quickly he gets things done, he always thinks he can do it faster than he can because he loses track of time passing. Nor does he remember his past experiences with similar projects. But I do, and after twenty years of waiting for him, I simply add 30 percent to his estimate, lessening our conflicts over time.

Is having a fluid approach to time bad? Not at all, unless (to quote a famous courier ad) you absolutely, positively have to get it there on time!

What's important to understand is that you relate to time *differently*, and it's worth respecting your differences and finding a middle ground where you both feel comfortable with the way things are getting done, including how quickly.

How Information Comes In

One of the things I find most remarkable about the brain is how it organizes information for us without our even realizing it. Like most people, I had not given this much thought, until I started contemplating the differences between how my brain functions compared to the brains of my family members with ADHD.

When I "receive" information, my brain puts it into a clear, focused hierarchy. I can be sitting at a park reading a book and focus on it, even though nearby a dog is chasing a cat, children are riding bikes, birds are singing, and a basketball game is going on. My brain filters out all the noise and distractions until I come to a point at which it makes sense to stop (because I see out of the corner of my eye that a basketball is flying my way or I come to the end of a chapter, for example). The same is true of ideas. When I hear or read a string of related ideas, my brain immediately "filters" them into a hierarchy.

What's most amazing is that I don't even know this is happening! I just "understand" that something deserves more focus than something else.

The ADHD brain receives information quite differently. Instead of being hierarchical, I like to think of it as "flat." Everything, important or not, initially receives about the same amount of attention. Noises, ideas, movements, even sometimes your own body parts, compete for attention at the same time in the ADHD brain. I have heard people with ADHD describe their brain as "noisy" (these are usually people who have tried medications and discovered that "noisy" is not the only way that brains can be). My daughter thinks of it as "open to lots of things," which is a wonderfully positive way to think about it.

One type is not inherently better than the other. My type of brain is really great in situations that require organization, such as the workplaces that I have chosen, writing books like this, and organizing a household with kids. An ADHD brain can be really great for creative activities, brainstorming, or high-adrenaline jobs with lots of equally important competing simultaneous information, such as working in an emergency room or being a police officer.

During courtship, the high-energy, flat, and not-very-organized brain of the ADHD spouse can fit right in. Remember how good your partner used to be at thinking of zany things to do, and how much fun it was to be spontaneous? You dropped everything and spent tons of time (and sometimes money) focused on each other. But after marriage, and particularly after having kids, many of your interactions shift to be more organizational in nature. There are bills to pay, kids to feed and educate, loans to pay off, and a home to maintain. The number of hours in the day remains the same, but your responsibilities have increased significantly. Most often, a non-ADHD spouse can make this transition easily, but the ADHD spouse ends up lost; and because the non-ADHD spouse assumes that an adult *should* be able to make the transition, this inability to adjust is frustrating.

"Flat" information processing has implications on what one sees and hears, what is memorable or not memorable, and how effectively one organizes. It's easy to see that someone whose brain automatically sorts information into a hierarchy will have an easier time of organizing than a person whose brain doesn't. Conversely, someone whose brain takes in everything at about the same level might be freed by that lack of hierarchy to think more easily outside the box.

But while some find lack of hierarchy a plus, far more find it difficult. One young man I know describes ADHD as "having a library in your head with no card filing system." Instead of feeling free to think outside the box, this man feels he can't rely on his own ability to process information accurately. He is so utterly capable of being wrong about things that his peers take for granted as common sense, that he is wary of opening his mouth. Those who don't know him perceive him as shy. He avoids engagement via withdrawal, sarcasm, or humor in order to cope with topics in which his disorganized mind and a lack of expertise put him at a disadvantage.

Excessive Shame

It is unfortunate that one of the recurring experiences for individuals with ADHD is personal criticism or comments about how they just did something stupid. Often, the people making these comments are important authority figures—parents, teachers, peers, bosses, and, yes, spouses.

Unfinished projects (distraction), poor decision making (impulsivity or too much information to process), memory problems, and more mean that people with ADHD often fail to do things *as quickly* as or *in the same way* that those without ADHD do them. Even if they are capable of finding resolution, they still "fail" relative to the non-ADHD standard. A great example of this is found in many schools, where smart but energetic kids can "fail" simply because they can't sit still.

The shame that people with ADHD, male or female, carry around with them after years and years of being told that they are inadequate is a critical factor when a marriage starts to fall apart, or when they are approached by a well-meaning spouse about asking for an evaluation for ADHD. Shame often triggers anger and defensiveness, which can shut down what ought to be a straightforward conversation before it has even begun. Anger, stonewalling, and defensiveness can seem unreasonable to a non-ADHD spouse who, not having experienced this same type of repeated bashing of the ego, doesn't understand it or interpret it correctly.

Fitting into the World

Today's world is one in which the pressure to assimilate, sort, and prioritize information is highly prized. The generally less directed approach that many with ADHD take is often seen as a deficiency. This is also true within the confines of marriage, particularly one in which both partners have significant time constraints and many responsibilities, such as taking care of children. While it may be interesting to explore the many ideas that come your way while you are supposed to be doing an errand, it is generally not *efficient* to do so. Most non-ADHD spouses cringe at the thought that it might take two hours to get gas, drop off the dry cleaning, or pick up some milk, because they know just how much more needs to be done before sunset.

Key to the success of many with ADHD is finding the "right life" in which to live. This means a job in which their particular talents for nonlinear thinking and quick emergency response are prized, and a spouse who can appreciate, or at least learn to live with, an often uneven distribution of work within the relationship. Without these things, many with ADHD feel that they don't really fit into the world, or that the face that they put forward in order to fit in is false.

The other critical factor for the success of an ADHD spouse in a relationship is for both partners to continue to respect differences and act on that respect. Here's what one woman with ADHD says about living a life in which others assume that "different" is not worthy of respect:

> I think [my husband] uses the ADD as an excuse to be bossy and stuff sometimes but I find it very upsetting and hard on my self esteem to have my disorder and learning disabilities used that way.
>
> We do have very different perspectives but reality is perspective. Just because I see things differently from someone else doesn't make one wrong or right…how I experience life is colored by my perception, it is what it is. I hate how people try to invalidate my thoughts feelings and perceptions because they are different from theirs. Like telling me [since] they feel…different[ly] from me [that their feelings] should make me magically change! It doesn't work that way. Even if my ADD makes me see or remember something "not right" it's still MY reality. It is like those movies where the hero has something crazy going on where they experience reality differently from everyone else.

In order to understand your differences and craft strategies to find common ground a couple must start with the basic assumption that each spouse's point of view is legitimately founded in that spouse's experiences. As such, it deserves respectful consideration. Understanding your spouse's quite different reality can be challenging, but it increases the likelihood you'll find a satisfying resolution to many of your conflicts. This is why so many negotiation experts suggest you take time to "walk a mile in your partner's shoes."

When You Both Have ADHD

There are plusses and minuses when both partners have ADHD. On the plus side, since both partners have experience with ADHD, it may be easier for them to be more compassionate towards, and aware of, the effort it takes to manage it. Further, if both of them are 'go with the flow' types, then a messy apartment or missed deadlines may not bother them much. Both partners may take joy in having adventures together.

It is also possible that one partner is more organized than the other, perhaps because that partner has been treating ADHD for longer, has less severe ADHD, or because that partner more readily takes on the 'it must be done even though it's boring' work. This can place a huge, stressful burden on that partner, who already has issues around ADHD to deal with and who may not be a naturally organized planner. As a result, dual ADHD couples can still fall into many of the negative patterns in this book, including the parent–child dynamics described later on.

Another area that can be more complicated for dual ADHD couples is that of employment. The vast majority of people with ADHD are gainfully employed, but the likelihood that there will be job problems, such as getting fired or quitting impulsively are increased for those who have ADHD. I also encounter some number of what I would call 'aspirational entrepreneurs' in my practice. These are people who want to work for themselves but don't have the organizational skills to get their business off the ground or sustain a fledgling business. They tend to drain the family bank and retirement accounts in pursuit of a dream that often doesn't pan out.

It's healthy to deal with ADHD openly in any relationship in which it is present, and particularly when both partners have it. Some strategies that I would recommend for dual-ADHD couples include:

- **Optimize ADHD treatment** for *both* partners in order to function to the best of teach person's ability. There is probably no 'natural organizer' in your partnership, so you both have to be able to pitch in on the boring stuff.
- **Seek strengths** – you will both have unique strengths that, if utilized, can help you thrive. It's not just about managing problems.

- **Educate yourselves well** about ADHD strategies, and about the unique challenges that women with ADHD face. I have information about this on my website and there are several good books on the topic.
- **Delegate…but not to each other!** Get as much assistance as you can afford, including regular or sporadic house cleaning, filing and paperwork, cooking, and more. You can even delegate to an electronic assistant – for example, asking it to add something to the shopping list it keeps on your phone so you don't have to dig around to find slips of paper. If you have a larger household, consider hiring an organizer once a year to help you sort through, and throw out, clutter.
- **Put bills on autopay**, then set reminders to check your bank balance regularly to avoid financial problems.
- **"Do" taxes all year long.** Have one box into which you throw only tax information, such as receipts and financial statements, all year long. I can't tell you how many people with ADHD I run into who are years behind on their taxes because it feels overwhelming to locate the information at the end of the year.
- **Find a career you love** that plays directly to your strengths. You'll be more likely to hold your job if you are interested in it or it feels like play.
- **Set a deadline for entrepreneurial ventures.** Chase your dreams, but be realistic about how long you can rely on the family savings before you create significant financial harm to those whom you care most about.
- **Put your treatment plan is in place before having kids**, if possible. Having young children is extremely stressful as there is 24/7 responsibility (much of it boring) and little sleep, which makes ADHD symptoms worse. The better you are managing your ADHD before your first child, the better you'll both do.

Finally, if you are a dual-ADHD couple, please ignore the labels of ADHD and non-ADHD in this book. Select the strategies that apply to you specifically, regardless of the label I use.

The Surprising Ways ADHD Symptoms Affect Your Marriage

"Nobody said it was easy
No one ever said it would be this hard
Oh take me back to the start . . ."
— "The Scientist," Coldplay

It's amazing how consistent are the patterns in struggling ADHD marriages. These patterns start with a common ADHD symptom that triggers a series of pretty predictable responses in both spouses, creating a downward spiral. But what if you knew what those triggers are, so that you could eliminate them or respond differently? What would happen if you could just say "Oh, that's the ADHD right there" and brush it off, rather than engage in battle? You can learn to recognize many of these patterns and then eliminate them from your relationship using methods that take ADHD into account.

Spoiler alert: You will see your relationship in this chapter, and you may have mixed emotions about it. On the one hand, if you're like many at our blog (www.adhdmarriage.com), you might feel relieved that someone is finally articulating what you have been experiencing and grateful to learn you are not alone. But these descriptions might also make you feel even sadder than you have been feeling. "What a waste!" you might think, or "This seems just hopeless!"

You should allow yourself to experience this sadness, because grieving for what you have not had in your marriage up to this point is one of the first steps toward building a new life together. But know that there are many reasons to be hopeful as well. As you learn about the patterns in ADHD relationships, you will also learn what to do about them.

Pattern 1 Painful Misinterpretations of ADHD Symptoms and Motives

Good communication isn't just a matter of saying the right words or starting your assumptions in the same places. Correct *interpretation* is critical, and in this realm couples dealing with ADHD may fail miserably for two basic reasons:

- An ADHD symptom is lurking that they don't realize is influencing their interaction (and subsequent interpretation of the interaction).
- They "live in the world" so differently that they incorrectly assume they understand the motives that are influencing frustrating behaviors.

One of the most common misinterpretations is feeling as if an ADHD spouse doesn't love his partner anymore because he isn't paying attention to her.

Take Maria. After five years of marriage, she wondered, "Why did I ever bother to get married? He doesn't even know I exist anymore!" During their courtship, Dan had been completely focused on her. But now she felt abandoned and ashamed that she no longer attracted her husband. She tried more and more desperately to get him to notice her. She started with sexier lingerie and new clothes, but that worked only for a while. She tried planning dates and sending cards, but he still didn't pay much attention. Frustrated, she turned to yelling at him, berating him, and demanding attention. Though this in-your-face approach forced Dan to pay attention in the short term, it drove him farther away over time. He took to retreating to his computer almost as soon as he came home, widening the distance between them. Because she was expressing herself so loudly, and he wasn't responding, Maria's resentment turned into full-blown anger.

What's going on here? Early on, Maria misinterpreted Dan's actions that were the result of his ADHD. One of the defining symptoms of ADHD is *distraction*. Dan had been able to temporarily hyperfocus on Maria during their courtship with the help of the brain chemicals released with infatuation, but once things settled down he reverted to showing his more typical ADHD symptoms. His distractibility meant that it was just as likely he would become interested in his dog, his computer, his car, or the soccer game as he would his wife. Things fell apart when she ascribed the negative emotion of dislike to the neutral act of distraction. "He doesn't love me anymore" was her fear, and every act of distraction served to reinforce this message in her mind.

If you had asked Dan during that period whether he still loved his wife, he would have looked at you in total confusion and said, "Of course!" Although his wife was at that very moment wallowing in despair over his treatment of her, he perceived things to be fine between them. This isn't because he is dense; it's just that after a lifetime of having people mad at or disappointed with him, Dan weathers periods of anger and criticism by mostly ignoring them. And, because people with ADHD don't receive and process information in a hierarchical way, Maria's suffering enters his mind at about the same level as everything else he perceives—the lights on the radio clock, the dog barking, the computer, the worrisome project he has at work.

"But wait!" you say. "It doesn't matter—she's still alone!" You would be right. Regardless of whether Dan was *intentionally* ignoring his wife or just distracted, actions speak louder than words. She becomes lonely and unhappy, and her needs must be addressed. But recognizing and then identifying the correct underlying problem is critical to finding the right solution. In marriage, just like in middle school math, if you pick the wrong problem to solve, you generally don't end up with a satisfactory result. Furthermore, the hurt caused by the incorrect interpretation that he no longer loves her elicits a series of bad feelings and behaviors that compound the problem. This is the critical dynamic of symptom–response–response at work.

Tips
Avoiding Misinterpretations of ADHD Symptoms and Motives

- **Learn all you can about ADHD** and how it manifests in adults. See the Resources section for useful material.

- **Assume you don't know your spouse's motives**. If something makes you feel bad, ask questions so you can better understand the underlying motives. Err on the side of too many questions so that you can reach an understanding. Keep the questions neutral. "Why did you take the dog for a walk right then?" or "Was the dog crossing her legs?!" are better approaches than "Is taking the dog out more important than finishing that chore I needed you to do?" or "I can't believe you ignored my request and played with the dog, instead!" Remember, tone of voice really matters.

- **Put measurements in place** to differentiate between actions and words. If you are feeling ignored, for example, you might keep track of the amount of time you spend together for a week. If you're actually spending time together but still feel ignored, quality may be the issue, not quantity.

- **Consider weekly "learning conversations"** (explained in detail in Step 4) to address issues that simply won't go away. Make it a point to discuss your motives and differences in approach that might be getting in the way of finding common ground.

- **Learn to laugh** when you miscommunicate, rather than see it as a sign that you'll never figure it out. Laughter reduces tension and helps keep you both in a positive mindset.

Pattern 2
The Destructive Symptom-Response-Response Cycle

The story of Dan and Maria illustrates another major theme in ADHD marriages: While the tendency is to blame ADHD for all of your problems, this is not actually the case. ADHD symptoms create unexpected, and often insidious, stresses on a marriage, as well as many misunderstandings. The destruction comes from a full pattern, though—one that includes the symptoms, the response to these symptoms, and then the response to that response.

Dan's distractibility was not, in itself, a destructive characteristic. It was the combination of Dan's symptom *and* Maria's specific interpretation of that symptom that amplified the issue so that it became part of a larger symptom-response-response cycle of problems.

One can imagine situations in which distractibility can be considered a plus—for example, if it was seen as the basis for creativity, or if it was simply accepted as an interesting part of one's personality (think creative scientist). Sometimes ADHD symptoms can be interpreted benignly as "eccentricities" or considered "annoying but acceptable" parts of an otherwise lovable personality.

I am not suggesting here that a non-ADHD spouse should simply roll over and say, "She's ignoring me because she's eccentric [or because she has ADHD]. Oh well!" In fact, having an ADHD spouse take charge of creating a systematic approach to treatment is one of the most important elements of improving your marriage. The "symptom" is, after all, at the beginning of the symptom-response-response sequence, and not much changes until the symptoms are under control—and that task can be accomplished only by the ADHD spouse.

ADHD in relationships is like a dance. One partner leads and initiates the steps, but *both* must understand their role to successfully circle the floor. An ADHD partner can address her symptoms, but the couple will be unsuccessful if the non-ADHD partner's response doesn't change, too.

As an example, imagine that Maria's response, rather than becoming angry and demanding, had been to say "Dan, I notice you've been particularly distracted for the last couple of weeks. I understand that, but I'm starting to feel a bit lonely as a result. How about if we go out for a date tomorrow?" He's delighted to go out. This completely different response to Dan's symptom results in quickly getting more attention, as well as a strengthening of therelationship overall. Dan still needs to improve his ability to attend to Maria in general, but a negative spiral of symptom-response-response has been avoided.

 Tips

Avoiding Symptom-Response-Response

- **Always consider the symptom *and* the response**. It's tempting to focus only on the ADHD issue when you confront a problem, but considering both the symptom and the response provides a more realistic picture of the situation and helps keep the ADHD partner from feeling as if she is being blamed.

- **Don't let the presence of negative responses turn into an excuse not to manage ADHD symptoms**. A classic example is the ADHD spouse who convinces himself that his wife's anger is the real cause of their problems. Yes, the anger is a factor that needs to be addressed, but it's also a response to specific ADHD symptoms.

- **Learn which responses produce positive outcomes**. Anger, nagging, and withdrawal are responses that don't move you forward. Look for different ways to get your ideas across. Responses are important, and choosing how to express yourself in constructive ways is the best and fastest way a non-ADHD partner can contribute to breaking out of symptom-response-response deadlocks.

Pattern 3
The Hyperfocus Courtship

One of the most stunning surprises about ADHD relationships is the transition from courtship to marriage. It is quite typical that a person with ADHD is so involved in and excited by courtship that he becomes hyperfocused on his partner. He lavishes attention on her, thinks of wonderful and exciting things to do together, and makes her feel as if she is the center of his world…which she is. Neither party is aware of what is going on, only their feelings that "this must be true love!" But when the hyperfocus stops, the relationship changes dramatically for both of them.

The best description I have read of this phenomenon was written by Jonathan Scott Halverstadt in his book *ADD & Romance: Finding Fulfillment in Love, Sex, and Relationships*. With his permission, I have excerpted it here:

> People with ADD seriously get into the stimulation of courting. In fact, you have never truly been courted and romanced until you have been courted and romanced by someone with ADD—someone who is hyperfocused on romancing you. This is the stuff Hollywood movies are made of. We're talking flowers and phone calls and picnics on the beach and poetry and billboards with messages of "I love you" and even skywriting. When someone with ADD is romancing you in the courting process, birds whistle a happier melody, angels sing, and air smells sweeter. Every day is a special day because you are both so much in love. When hyperfocused on romance, men and women with ADD do the most fabulous, sweet, loving, nurturing things—because it is stimulating.
>
> Yes, they do it because it is stimulating for *them*. They don't do it because their partner will enjoy it, although that certainly is part of the reason they do it.

But the biggest reason they sweep you off your feet with this incredible display of affection is because they are doing it for themselves, to self-medicate their brains with endorphins. They aren't trying to be selfish or self-centered. But they do all this courting and romancing to the hilt because it feels good for them to be stimulated by the excitement of romance. Mind you, this "it feels good" aspect is not just about your average "it makes me feel good to do something nice for the one I love." Also included in this mix is "I feel better in my own body"—a general, overall sense of well-being the person with ADD may not experience on a day-to-day basis like most of the population....

The person on the receiving end of this courting process doesn't realize that most of this attraction has less to do with them than they think. In fact, they usually think it's all about them. And why wouldn't they?

But the ADD person wouldn't be able to tell you it's about self-medicating either. They are clueless as to why they're so enthralled with their newfound love. All they know is that the feelings they are having are so intense, so wonderful, that this person has to be their soul mate. They are in no way conscious of the self-medicating aspect of what they are doing.

Unfortunately, the ADD partner goes on and on with all this exciting courtship stuff until it becomes a commonplace experience. And when it loses its newness—when it is no longer stimulating—it simply stops. Sometimes immediately. One day they're full of love, birds and angels singing and all, and the next day nothing. Gone. Zilch. Zero.

When the thrill is gone, the thrill is gone. The ADD partner no longer writes the poetry or the songs or sends romantic phone messages because they aren't getting the rush anymore. And when it isn't stimulating to them

> anymore, they simply stop those behaviors and move on to something else. They may, in fact, be very much in love with their partner, but the stimulation is gone. In order to feel better—okay in their own body—they've got to find something else that is stimulating....
>
> Of course the object of all the previous attention and affection is usually stunned at this point. Up to this point, their mate has been more than they had ever dreamed of. Then, suddenly, he or she just isn't there anymore. The non-ADD partner ends up sitting in the dust of an illusion asking themselves what went wrong. They are confused. They are hurt. They are bewildered. And they are angry.
>
> Amazingly, the ADD partner is also feeling confused by this time, too. Here they thought they had found the mate of their dreams. This was the most stimulating relationship they had ever been in. Then, suddenly, those feelings were gone. If they were married during this intense courtship phase—which often happens—then both partners could be panicking at this point.[7]

I tell you about hyperfocused courtships because the transition to "normal" life can be so confusing and hurtful. The turning off of hyperfocus is dramatic. Almost inevitably, the non-ADHD spouse takes it personally. As an example, my husband stopped hyperfocusing on me the *day* we came home from our honeymoon. Suddenly, he was gone—back to work, back to his "regular" life. I was left behind completely. Within six months of my wedding day, I was seriously questioning whether I had married the right man.

He wasn't a different person—he was still sweet, thoughtful (when he thought of me, which wasn't often), smart...he just wasn't paying *any* attention. I was sure I had done something wrong or was not attractive to him anymore, now that I had been officially

7. Halverstadt, Jonathan Scott, *ADD & Romance: Finding Fulfillment in Love, Sex, & Relationships*, Taylor Publishing (now transferred to Rowman & Littlefield), 1998, pp. 51-53.

"conquered." In retrospect, I know that my insecurity had nothing to do with reality. He loved me deeply. He just didn't realize that he wasn't paying attention because he was distracted by just about everything else.

And therein lies the solution to the hyperfocus issue. If you are engaged to a person with ADHD who has romanced you and focused on you, expect that this will come to an end—perhaps abruptly. And when it does, don't look to yourself as the reason for the change. It is the result of ADHD symptoms and dopamine returning to normal (i.e. low) levels, and nothing more. Knowing this, the two of you can work on figuring out what other stimulating things you can do together that will keep the spark alive. Accept that ADHD is a factor, then push it aside by consciously and unabashedly making time for romance a top priority.

If you have already experienced the confusion and hurt of a hyperfocused courtship coming to an end, you are probably harboring resentment, anger, and anxiety. Give yourselves the benefit of the doubt; assume that you *are* with the right person and that the qualities that attracted you to each other still remain. It's just that the two of you have experienced a surprising shock without much guidance as to how to respond to it. Thinking this way can help you move through your hurt and anger to a better understanding of your mutual feelings.

My husband and I had never heard of ADHD or of hyperfocus, so our hurt continued for quite some time. For me, it turned into a festering resentment about being ignored, which was very destructive. This resentment is a good example of the symptom-response-response syndrome found in ADHD relationships. My husband's symptom "distraction" led to a response (my loneliness and resentment). My resulting surliness induced a response to the reaction (anger and retreat by my husband). Under it all, though, remained an ADHD symptom: distraction. At its core, my husband needed to treat his ADHD. I needed to encourage that effort.

Tips
Dealing with Hyperfocus Courtship Shock

- **Remember that it's not personal.** Hyperfocus courtship followed by an abrupt ending is a well-documented part of many ADHD relationships. The non-ADHD spouse will benefit most by internalizing that it's not personal, even though it feels that way, and forgiving the ADHD spouse.
- **Improve connections**. Feeling ignored is still painful. Address the issue head-on by establishing ways to improve your connections and intimacy.
- **Allow yourself to mourn** for the pain the ADHD hyperfocus shock has caused you both. This will help you move past it.

Pattern 4
The Parent–Child Dynamic

The most common and most destructive of all of the patterns I will describe is the parent–child dynamic, where one spouse is almost always responsible and the other rarely is. Here's how it usually starts: Symptomatically, an untreated ADHD spouse does not follow up on tasks for which he is responsible. He intends to, and says he will, but he simply gets distracted or forgets. At first his wife compensates and takes over the lion's share of the responsibility, but soon she resents the burden this places on her. She gets to do all of the scutwork, while he "cruises along" and does "the fun stuff."

When approached about his lapses, he agrees to help out, but rarely follows through. She reminds him again; he agrees again; he forgets again. His actions aren't intentional; he's simply distracted and unfocused. Over time he becomes "reliably unreliable" in his wife's eyes, and she begins to nag and attack him in order to get him to "pay attention to what he should be doing and stop goofing off." He retreats from the attack; she attacks harder in the face of his retreat. Soon, they both learn that interaction is painful: an exercise in being hurt, and feeling hurt. The only way she seems to be able to get his attention is to blow up at him. Hopelessness, frustration, and anger set in.

Sometimes he does get things done. But his wife learns to be wary because he is so inconsistent. What she will remember is not his accomplishments, but his failures—and she behaves accordingly. He learns that getting things done doesn't get him much credit, which demotivates him.

Compounding this downward spiral, people from outside the marriage may observe that the ADHD spouse is "lots of fun" and "wonderful," while the non-ADHD spouse comes across as seeming cranky, unappreciative of her "wonderful" spouse, and more and more unreasonable. She appears disillusioned and bad tempered, so others, including family members, may start to blame her for the couple's issues. They may start wondering, "What's wrong with her?" and "Why hasn't he divorced her yet?" These attacks further increase her resentment and reinforce that he "gets away" with being irresponsible, while she gets no credit for picking up the messes he leaves behind. Simultaneously, her husband may start to listen to those around them and agree: his wife is being unreasonable. This makes him resistant to taking responsibility for his ADHD, or for making the effort necessary to do any of those pesky chores.

Parent–Child Plus Kids

Taking care of kids is so time intensive that it puts extra emphasis and importance on staying organized and "getting things done" and can exacerbate parent–child pattern issues. In addition, once a non-ADHD spouse feels her husband is unreliable, she can lose confidence in his competency to safely take care of their children. "What happens if he drives too fast when the kids are in the car?" she wonders, or "Will he really be there to pick them up after their lessons, or will they be left standing on the curb, easy prey for strangers?" "What if he never gets around to feeding our young children lunch?" These fears go to the heart of what she cares about most. She starts to pull the kids closer to her (and away from him) to protect them from the interruptions and disappointments created by her spouse's ADHD symptoms. In some households, life becomes a noticeable "us vs. him."

Verbal Abuse from the "Parent"

Feeling that there is little left to lose, and seething with anger and resentment, the non-ADHD spouse can start to belittle and humiliate her spouse privately, and often publicly. "Why can't you do anything right?" and "You're worthless" are common refrains in the parent–child adult relationship. Though he may fight back, the ADHD spouse struggles deeply as the recipient of this abuse, because it sounds like so many comments he has heard throughout his life from other "authority" figures such as parents, relatives, teachers, and coaches. He may become understandably defensive, but this only further infuriates his wife.

What follows is an example of extreme verbal abuse from our blog. I include it here because this ADHD man describes so well the paralysis that people with ADHD feel after being on the receiving end of this vicious cycle. His example, while extreme, is far from uncommon:

> Now anything I do related to my ADHD (or not) is met with ridicule and scorn. I hear things like "You're such an idiot" or "You can't get anything right, I hate you!" I understand she is frustrated. When I tell her she is being hurtful she replies with "How do you think I feel? I've been dealing with your sorry self for sixteen years!" I now feel as if I am walking on thin ice. I'm afraid to say anything in fear of an argument. On the other hand saying nothing does not help either.... When I look back on our marriage, this is nothing new. Almost from the beginning my ADHD must have played a role. Anytime I spoke, my thoughts or ideas were put down. Any task I performed was met with, "Why did you do it that way?" or "This isn't right at all, what's the matter with you!" This has made me go into seclusion within myself (if that makes sense). I'm not open at home. I'm silent, expressionless. It has made me less in touch with my children, too. I am never sure what I should say or do with them. I find myself missing the boat so to speak. Another day goes by and I didn't help my daughters with their trumpet music. I didn't help my daughter with her track aspirations. I didn't help my

> daughter with her project that's due in days. Then I'm told things like "You are useless, I can do a lot better without you."

This man experiences his wife's disdain and verbal abuse with retreat and a continued loss of self-confidence. He is isolated from his children and feels hopeless and incapable. His angry wife may see her own actions as something that he has "earned" and a way of shaming him out of his retreat, as well as the only way to get his attention. Blinded by her anger, she may not even care about the damage she is inflicting. The net effect, though, is that they have both become paralyzed, and he is traumatized.

You may recognize signs of verbal abuse in your own relationship. The first step to controlling this is to decide that verbal abuse is not an acceptable outlet for anger. While it may feel good to get back at your spouse, the inevitable result of verbal abuse is that both spouses are deeply hurt. It's hard to believe that the wife above would wish to further paralyze her spouse, but that is just what has resulted from her abuse. Furthermore, the abuse (and his response to it) does nothing to help her deal with her anger. She remains miserable, and so does he. Unless the abuse stops immediately, they will both need professional counseling, and fast.

I have been in this exact phase myself, and I will talk in much greater depth about how to manage paralyzing chronic anger.

The Parent–Child Dynamic Creates Hopelessness in the Non-ADHD Spouse, Too

The anguish that the parent–child pattern brings to the non-ADHD spouse is expressed differently, but is just as real. Here are two typical examples:

> [Everything] seemed manageable before we had children. I could live with managing work, his schedule, all the shopping, bills, etc. We had several blowouts about his inattentiveness to me, his tendency to choose his friends over me, broken promises, etc. But I never thought that was ADHD. I thought I had unreasonable expectations, perhaps

> I was too needy. He even told me once I was not as independent as he thought when he first dated me. I think independent meant not needing anything from him in the way of follow-through, or respect, or consideration. At any rate, we've certainly been arguing more and more as of late.
>
> We have two small children, so exiting this marriage is not something I would prefer to do. I love him, but I have to be honest here. I have years of pent-up frustration at his behavior. He can be amazingly inconsiderate, he doesn't offer to help unless asked…He cannot anticipate how to be considerate. In short, I feel many times like the mom of three children instead of two. I have to keep his schedule as well as my own and the kids. I have to do all the shopping, financials, pretty much all organizational issues. If I want him to do something I have to nag repeatedly, and he may well act like a petulant teenager when I do ask. I cannot express frustration at him—that is not allowed. If I do, I am guilty of disrespecting him. If he has let me down by another broken promise, I am overreacting and love to fight. I feel trapped.

Another woman wrote:

> Because of my husband's irresponsibility, he ended up ruining my credit twice. I am often stuck with having to buy all the groceries and covering for his share of the rent (because either his job messed up his paycheck or he was having problems with his bank account). It's always something and I'm so sick and tired of the excuses, whether they're valid or not. I hear so many excuses that I've pretty much become numb to his endless tales of woes. Communication is a major problem in our marriage. He doesn't listen very well and it's frustrating when I learn that he didn't pay attention to key points, especially in matters pertaining to the finances. It's like he zones in and out to keep up with the conversation….
>
> He's very forgetful and I hate having to constantly remind him to take care of important matters as if he were a child. I have lost nearly all respect for him. It's like I have three

> children (instead of two). I resent what he has put me through...I'm getting stressed out all the time and I'm currently suffering from severe anxiety attacks, including high blood pressure.

The anger and anxiety that these women feel as they deal with their spouses' untreated ADHD symptoms color every aspect of how they live. The second was actually on medical leave due to stress as this book was being written. They pick up extra tasks when their spouse does not do them—bills, chores, basic cooking, cleaning, and organization—but the pressure this creates is intense. They also start to question themselves. *Am I too needy? How can I feel this numb? Why can't I get past this frustration? Can I ever trust him?* Worst of all, they exude a sense of hopelessness. Both of the women above are currently considering divorce.

Sometimes, as the negativity of the parent–child dynamic intensifies, a non-ADHD woman actually *overcompensates* for her spouse's lack of follow-through. This results from her anger and from her increasing feelings that she needs to "teach" her spouse to do (and be) better. So, for example, a countertop left dirty in the kitchen after dinner becomes yet more proof of her husband's inadequacy, rather than something that can be handled with little effort the next morning with the breakfast dishes. To prove that he is inadequate, and teach him that it ought to be done, she feels she *must* show him that the counter must be cleaned now. So she does it, even though she could leave it for later, and even though she is extremely tired. To make sure her retreating husband gets the message, she tells him he didn't finish his job. But that reminder, rather than inspiring him to do better next time, demotivates him—and not only on the topic of countertops. "I'll never be able to please you," he thinks, and tomorrow he just isn't interested in trying again—at anything.

Why "Parenting" a Spouse Is Different from Parenting a Child with ADHD

Like many parents, my first experience with an ADHD diagnosis came through my child. My approach was to help my daughter in any way I could. I learned everything I could about ADHD, talked with her doctor, and worked with her school to make sure she received the assistance she needed. At her doctor's recommendation, we let her make the decision about whether to take medications (she didn't want to for about two years, until school got harder). I spent lots of time sitting with her while she did homework, trying to keep her focused, and "helping" to direct her life.

One of the benefits of a childhood diagnosis of ADHD is that you and your child often feel as if you are "making progress," in part because kids naturally change and move forward as they grow up. This provides positive reinforcement for the parent who helps the child. "Okay, it was a struggle, but look what she can do now!" you think. Another benefit is that kids naturally listen to what their parents have to say (at least when they are younger). For the most part, they are interested in being in your good graces. One of your jobs as a parent is to establish structure for your child. All kids need loving structure and welcome it. Kids with ADHD need it even more.

When your child struggles with the symptoms of ADHD, your heart goes out to her. You ache for her and wish that she would have an easier time of it. You are also ready to celebrate every victory that comes her way in obvious and noisy fashion. In short, you "parent" your child—overtly and protectively. But the things that you do to support your child are not so good for your marital relationship. Your spouse does not generally want you to tell him what to do or structure his life, nor does he look to you for wisdom.

Adults don't have the same growth momentum that children do to help enable and amplify progress. In adults, change comes from hard work, not getting a year older. This means that an ADHD spouse seems more prone to get "stuck" than a child does, and do things over and over again, which is just the opposite of what you would expect: you expect the *adult* to be able to progress, and the *child* to get stuck. Non-ADHD spouses tend not to take into account how hard it is to make big changes as an adult, particularly if they are simultaneously observing a child's progress.

Forward momentum isn't the only issue. It is an adult's job to "parent" a child. The child expects this, and so do you. This makes both of you in tune with your role. However, one of a partner's jobs is to romantically support a spouse. Your spouse does not expect you to parent him, and will likely resent it if you do. Furthermore, if you parent your spouse, you will lose the romance of your marriage, as it's almost impossible to be sexually attracted to a parent figure.

To make matters worse, while you ache at each and every one of your child's failures, your frustration with a lack of progress by your ADHD spouse more often leads to anger than empathy. The not-so-subtle difference in your feelings is communicated clearly through actions, body language, and tone of voice. Rather quickly, the ADHD spouse starts to believe that you don't love him. For any non-ADHD spouse, it's much harder not to criticize the continuation of ADHD symptoms when they are exhibited by an adult "who should know better" than by a child who is "still learning."

Almost all of the ADHD spouse's shortcomings directly increase the workload of the non-ADHD spouse, particularly around the house, which is why this is such an area of conflict. If he doesn't pick things up, she feels she has to. If he doesn't pay the bills, she must, or the electricity gets turned off. If he doesn't mix well at parties, neither of them gets invited. If he doesn't shovel the walk...you get the picture. This isn't the case as frequently with kids with ADHD. If a child is socially awkward, most parents don't suffer the consequences. A child who doesn't finish his homework is a concern, but the parents know that their daughter will only need help remembering homework until she either gets her reminder system straightened out or until she graduates from school. Also, many parents get assistance with their child's learning differences through school resource programs and individualized education programs (IEPs). Others are assisting, and there is a *perceived end* to the help you will need to provide a child in addition to the dovetailing of expectations around your mutual roles. As the quotes earlier in this chapter demonstrate, there is no help for, and no perceived end to, the dysfunction of a parent–child adult conflict.

If there is only one thing that you take away from this book, I hope it is that the parent-child dynamic *cannot* continue. There are many healthy ways to be heard, balance your relationship, and get things done when you are impacted by ADHD. Parent-child dynamics is not one of them.

Tips
Avoiding the Parent–Child Dynamic for the Non-ADHD Spouse

- **Take control of *your own* actions, and stop all verbal abuse immediately**. The lack of respect verbal abuse communicates makes improving your marriage virtually impossible. Find a different outlet for your frustration.

- **Don't nag!** Although it feels right now as if the only way you can get your spouse's attention is to nag or parent, don't do it! Keep searching for alternatives. Use family meetings to organize and discuss your issues with less distraction; consult with a marriage therapist; schedule dates to connect. You are right to insist that attention be paid to you; just work with your spouse to find more productive ways to get that attention than nagging.

- **Recognize that you can *never* successfully "parent" a spouse**, even though it's possible to successfully help a child with ADHD. "Parenting" an ADHD spouse is always destructive to your relationship because it demotivates and generates frustration and anger. As you look for ways to live together successfully, always ask the question, "Am I moving into a parenting role with these words or actions?" If so, reject or modify that option. (Note here: This doesn't mean you can't ever be involved with your spouse's ADHD; it just means that you need to be conscious of *how* you are involved.)

- **Remember that parenting a spouse kills the romance** and warm feelings critical to a successful marriage.

- **Applaud all forward progress.** Research shows that encouragement, support, and recognition of success are far more effective than offering "help" when your goal is to inspire continued success.

- **Understand that offers of "help" can be misconstrued** in adult parent–child relationships. They may say, "You're not competent enough to do this alone." Try to offer partnership: that is, participate in creating solutions that work for you both rather than "fix" something your spouse isn't doing right.
- **Develop verbal cues**. Arrange with your spouse a method for pointing out and talking about parent–child interactions as they happen, so you can start to identify them. Remain as neutral as possible during these interactions. Your goal is to stop parent–child interactions and replace them with more effective and constructive interactions. See Step 4 later in this book for more information about verbal cues.
- **Keep your marriage at the top of your list**. If you have a child with ADHD, make sure to keep the needs of your marriage up front. You'll find time for your child, but it's all too easy to lose track of your relationship.
- **Consider hiring professional help**. This is a very difficult dynamic to change. A professional ADHD coach or therapist can help you identify parent–child interactions and provide ideas for new ways to interact. *Make sure the person has experience with ADHD!*

Tips
Avoiding the Parent–Child Dynamic for the ADHD Spouse

If you are a spouse with ADHD, the development of a parent–child pattern means that you are not fully treating your ADHD in a way that effectively supports your role in your marriage. You may be tempted to ignore my statement about this, and counter that your spouse is too picky or demanding. This may be true in part, but higher standards are often a response to an ADHD spouse not taking enough responsibility in the partnership. When the ADHD spouse gains better control of ADHD symptoms and becomes more reliable in the eyes of his partner, the standards relax. The nagging also diminishes significantly. So, I'll reiterate: *If you are being parented, it means that ADHD symptoms are getting in the way of your relationship, whether you are aware of it or not.*

To get out of parent–child dynamics, consider these suggestions:

- **Talk with your doctor about improving treatment**. You may wish to change medication dosage or timing, undertake a regular exercise routine, do mindfulness training, or adopt behavioral changes through cognitive behavioral therapy, ADHD coaching, or another approach. It's critical that the ADHD partner become more reliable.
- **Start with something symbolic.** Take full ownership of a project or task that is meaningful to your non-ADHD spouse. Don't assume you know what this is; ask, and listen. (Hint: as the two of you discuss what you should take on, make sure you choose a meaningful task that fits with your strengths, not your weaknesses. I can't tell you how many people with ADHD I've heard from who decide this means they should pay the bills, even though there is ample proof that financial management is one of their weakest skills.) Figure out all the steps. Develop a reminder system so you get it done at the right times. Achieving success by taking on this symbolic project is the first step in getting your spouse to calm down a bit and move ahead again.
- **Determine what you are *not* good at** and establish a plan for getting it done by someone else. *Don't* hand it to your spouse, who is already overburdened, unless he agrees that you are taking at least as much of his burden away from him by taking on some of his tasks.
- **Start a regular exercise program** if you don't have one already. This will improve your health, energy, and focus. It will also improve your mood, and therefore your interactions with your spouse. (Note: The focus benefit of exercise lasts for a few hours, so thinking about *when* you exercise can help you use this tool to its best advantage.)

- **Agree to verbal cues** to point out parent–child interactions as they happen. "Cue" responses such as "Please don't talk to me that way" can gently alert your partner that the direction of the conversation needs to change.
- **Improve your sleep routine.** See ADHDmarriage.com for a worksheet that can help you do it.

Pattern 5 The Chore Wars

Unfortunately, having a spouse with untreated ADHD can translate into a lot of extra work for a non-ADHD spouse. In fact, if the partners don't get workload distribution issues under control, the anger and resentment that builds up can end the marriage.

Divorce over whether the chores are getting done?! It sounds silly until you realize that for the non-ADHD spouse, the ADHD partner's lack of participation in household chores becomes *symbolic* of all of the things that person doesn't do in the marriage "in the normal way." For many, not helping out also communicates a lack of respect and caring.

Furthermore, all those chores are exhausting, not to mention never ending. Feeling as if one is "forced" to do all of them because nobody else will makes the non-ADHD spouse feel like a slave. The insult of this is only compounded when an ADHD spouse confronted with her lack of participation answers, "I just can't remember to do that stuff!" or says "Sure, I'll do it," but then doesn't do it (again)! One of the most frustrating insults of all is to shrug it off with, "People with ADHD aren't good at chores," and not try to figure out how to do better.

Okay, people with *untreated* ADHD often aren't that great at chores. They can have trouble initiating things that don't have high interest value. They need stimulation to stay involved. Chores, of course, are way down on everyone's list on both counts.

Treatment helps people with ADHD focus and makes it easier to create reminder systems, initiate new tasks, and stay with something even if it is boring. I have no statistical information on this, but my observation is that people with ADHD have to work harder than people without ADHD to accomplish the same boring chore. Whether it's someone who has to take the extra step of setting a timer to be able to start cleaning the kitchen, or a person who must organize a desk in a certain way in order to stay focused enough to write a letter, people with ADHD seem to take more steps to get the same thing done. Often just getting their brains to calm down enough to take on a chore is a challenge.

Whether or not it takes extra effort, the bottom line is that the ADHD spouse still needs to pitch in. Helping out in some way is critical to communicating to your spouse, "I care about you and us, and I also take pride in our home."

Sometimes, people with ADHD feel that they *are* doing chores. Here is a post from a recently married man who is struggling with his wife's inattention to the housework:

> I've been married for a year to a wife with diagnosed ADHD (since childhood) who is very comfortable with her diagnosis and feels she has a very firm grasp and control of her condition…since we have moved in, she has never cleaned up her things, she still has not unpacked from a trip two months ago. I do everything I can to keep everything I own put away and clean. We made a job list a few months back of who is responsible for what. I do mine consistently and to her nagging specifications, while she has yet to do the bulk of her jobs. She is currently unemployed, but when I come home from eight hours, I honestly cannot tell anything has been done. She occasionally will do one small task, but on the whole nothing happens. I try and talk with her…but I always get told she is very busy and gets things done. The one time I didn't do my job for the week I got a lecture on how we both need to do our jobs.
>
> Any time I try and help or even suggest something with ADHD it ends up ugly…I really don't know what to do…I am terrified what will happen when we have children and she runs our household. I have no problem

> working and helping with chores but I'm working full time, doing all the chores, I cook every meal and…I'm usually the one in the doghouse.

Unbalanced responsibilities around the house are creating the problem here, but a bigger issue is emerging: as their dysfunction around chores increases, the non-ADHD spouse is beginning to fear the future and to lose trust in their ability to cope together.

This one may actually end up as "divorce over the chores," though you can see that the symptom-response-response pattern makes it more complex than "just" chores. This couple would benefit from a third party to mediate their dispute and they should put objective measurements in place. Are the chores getting done or not? Are the chores he's requesting reasonable? These things can be measured. Use the Chore Score Worksheet in the Worksheets and Tools section to measure who's doing what and how burdensome it is.

Here's another example:

> I have been with my husband for the last eleven years. When we met, he was very attentive to me. He was fun to hang out with, always had ideas of fun stuff to do, told good jokes, and helped me, for the first time in my life, to learn to relax some. It was wonderful!
>
> Now, though, I have to handle ALL the finances because when my husband took care of our finances, he didn't balance the checkbook for six months! He thought that whatever the bank said was in our account was the amount we had—regardless of how many outstanding checks there were. I have our son with me every minute that I am not teaching (partially because of my husband's schedule). That includes doctor appointments, dentist appointments, Cub Scouts, sports, homework, bedtime routines, getting ready for school, parent-teacher conferences, etc. I have to take care of all household chores because my husband forgets to do them or gets distracted in the middle of them. I plan all of our meals because my

> husband can't/doesn't/won't plan for a week at a time. I do all the grocery shopping because my husband buys random things that "sound good" instead of sticking to a list, and I end up cooking almost all of the meals.
>
> It is EXTREMELY STRESSFUL to feel like there is no companionship because I can't rely on my husband to do what he said he would do. It is sooo lonely to feel like my husband is constantly in his own "happy place" while I am saddled with all of the responsibility…I, the non-ADD spouse, am hurt/upset/frustrated angry/overwhelmed by all the responsibilities that I feel like I carry alone, and others [outside the marriage] don't understand. Most of the time, I feel like I have all the responsibilities while he has all the fun!!

Non-ADHD spouses who find themselves in this situation often add to their problems by personally taking on too many of the chores that are cast aside early in their relationship. It's generally more efficient to do this but it hurts the relationship in the long run. For couples just starting out, it's better to take the time, effort, and, yes, conflict to get into the habit of creating a satisfying distribution of chores early on, rather than to let one spouse shoulder most of the work. Later, the addition of children or more stressful jobs can make continuing that unbalanced pattern a physical impossibility, and at that point you're so busy you don't have time to find the right compensation strategies for the ADHD spouse to help out.

For the woman above, the real issue is captured in these two ideas: "It is extremely stressful to feel like there is no companionship" and "I can't rely on my husband to do what he said he would do. It is sooo lonely…." His lack of follow-through, even though it is a result of an ADHD symptom and not a reflection of how he feels, symbolizes to this wife that her spouse doesn't care about her or respect her. She's lonely. She's frustrated she can't change things, even if she "backs off":

> Yes I am a nag at times and yes I hate it. But I feel forced into this position. I feel like I have tried SOO many

> things. When a project comes up, I let him set the due date and promise not to bring it up until that date has passed with the project still undone—just allows more projects to accumulate undone as far as I can see. And I am that much angrier it is still undone.

Loneliness, fear, respect issues, and sheer exhaustion seem to be at the heart of most chore wars. Anger is the result.

Tips

Getting Around the Chore Wars

- **Constant nagging is a warning indicator** that ADHD is hurting your marriage—a lot. Don't just brush it off. Look to find problematic underlying ADHD symptoms, don't just assume the non-ADHD spouse is being unreasonable.
- **Quit nagging, cold turkey.** If you're already entrenched in the chore wars and nagging has become a habit, look for more constructive ways to express your needs. For the ADHD spouse on the receiving end of the nagging, it's not just about what chores get done; it's also about who is in charge of his life, making nagging much more destructive than you might think.
- **Measure the extent of your problem** using the Chore Score Worksheet in the Worksheets and Tools section at the back of this book. Use the information on the worksheet to engage in some learning conversations (see Step 4) to talk about your discoveries from the week. Both spouses need to be aware of the symbolic nature of these battles in order to make it a priority to stop fighting over chores.
- **Think treatment.** At the heart of most chore wars is at least one ADHD symptom. It might be distraction, inability to initiate, inability to complete tasks, or something else. Figure out which one (or more) it is, and treat it.

- **Get on the same page** when it comes to who does what and when. Try the Recipe for Success system in the back of the book or set up your own electronic system.
- **Don't overcompensate** for a spouse's untreated ADHD. Even though it may be more efficient in the short term, it's better to continue to pursue negotiations that lead to a more even distribution of labor and reduction in ADHD symptoms than to endure the resentment that taking on all of the chores engenders.
- **Think in terms of "well enough."** Most chores don't have to be done to perfection; "well enough" will do. This helps prevent one or both spouses feeling as if they are being held to "nagging specifications."

Pattern 6
The Blame Game

The Blame Game. Sounds like the name of a TV show. "All right, for 40 points: who didn't take out the garbage this week?"

But it's not a game at all. Put simply, the blame game is corrosive. As long as you are spending time blaming the other person, you'll never thrive.

The blame game goes something like this: With parent–child dynamics in place and/or chore wars exhausting them, both spouses become mired in resentment and anger. A non-ADHD wife starts to blame her ADHD husband for her unhappiness, either because he doesn't admit his ADHD is an issue or because he's not doing enough to control it. "He says he's trying, but I don't see any changes; I just hear words. And words aren't enough!" The more she blames him, the more his behavior seems to reinforce her "right" to blame him. "See?" she asks. "That's exactly what I mean. He never [fill in the blank]. Things will never change."

At the same time, the ADHD spouse finds that his wife is not behaving at all as he expected she would. She berates and belittles him, complains, criticizes things that never seemed to bother her while they were dating, and doesn't appreciate all of the hard work he devotes to supporting the family. He can't figure out why his wife used to accept him and love him for who he is, and now acts as if she can't stand him.

She blames him for their misery. He blames her for ruining their relationship with her anger or coldness. As long as one or both of you is playing the blame game, nothing will improve. The person who is doing the blaming doesn't look inward enough to take responsibility for changes that he or she can contribute to your mutual well-being:

> As far as the implosion of the marriage is concerned, [my husband] sees [his] ADHD as a non-issue, and has pinned everything on me. When I mean "everything," this even includes "things that never happened," "things I didn't do or say," and "things he did but doesn't remember properly, so he assumes I did them." I've also been told that all sorts of really horrible things he did (including physical injuries that occurred due to his inattention) he *didn't* do, and that I'm a liar....
>
> I've been scapegoated and bad-mouthed by him to his therapist and family....It hurts more than I can describe to think that people I love believe I'm a horrible person because they've been handed a fictional account of our marriage.

This is an extreme example. But if you find that you and your spouse are keeping tabs on who's doing what (and who isn't), or if you're badmouthing each other to friends and relatives, you are participating in the blame game.

I personally think the word *blame* should be banned in the realm of marriage. Chronic blame does a great deal of harm:

- It creates an environment in which the experimentation needed to change adult behaviors becomes "dangerous." You fail, you get blamed.
- It shifts the focus away from the blamer, making that person less likely to reflect on his or her own contributions to the issues.

- It diminishes each partner's ability to be empathetic.
- It impairs the ability to forgive.
- It sets two people up as adversaries, rather than partners.
- It builds resentment in both partners. The chemicals that your brain makes in response to resentment (unlike those made in response to anger) take a long time to go away, poisoning the atmosphere in which you interact.
- It provides an excuse not to try harder. ("Why bother? I'll never be good enough" or "If I try, then I'll be admitting I'm the one to blame.")

What's the best way out of the blame game? To decide to stop playing it. Consider the words of one woman who did just that:

> My relationship has had its ups and downs, and in the beginning, I blamed my ADD partner. Once I began to learn about ADD and how the mind of an ADD person worked, I was intrigued and very irritated with myself. I realized that a lot of my reactions and actions towards him were negative in every sense of the word. I used to get so frustrated that tasks weren't completed, or they were forgotten, or they took too long to be accomplished. One day I thought to myself, "in the end, being frustrated over a task, is it really worth it?" To me, even though I felt I was taking on more responsibility, I still felt that it wasn't worth the daily battles, let alone the aggravation.
>
> Strangely, coming to this realization brought me some internal peace. I stopped caring about what wasn't done, and started noticing the things that were done. I also acknowledge that ADD or not, he can't read my mind. I started giving him more positive reinforcement to encourage the good habits rather than the not-so-good habits. I feel that this has been a more constructive way to approaching him, rather then constantly complaining. The more I complained, the worse things got. It was

demotivating [for him]...now we are working towards brainstorming better approaches.

This woman's ability to see her own role in their issues hasn't fixed everything, but it has brought her more peace, a stronger appreciation of her spouse, and, she reports, a gradual move by both of them toward "middle ground." In addition, her husband finally feels that it is safe to start to work together to develop better approaches. Because she was able to stop blaming him, they are now better partners in their marriage.

Tips
Getting Out of the Blame Game

- **Look inward**. In an ADHD relationship, it's almost certain that both spouses are contributing to marital problems, often in specific patterns. Openly accepting your own responsibility and accepting the validity of the other spouse's complaints (even if you don't understand their underpinnings) can quickly take some of the pressure off.

- **Don't equate good intentions with good outcomes**. Actions are important, and if one spouse says either's actions are inadequate, they likely are, regardless of the intent.

- **Differentiate each spouse from his or her symptoms**. That means ADHD spouse from ADHD symptoms, such as distractibility and disorganization, *and* the non-ADHD spouse from "symptoms" such as nagging, anger, or hopelessness. When you do this you make room for yourselves to "attack" the problem together without attacking an individual and putting that person on the defensive.

- **Work with a counselor who knows ADHD**. If you are working with a professional counselor, make sure that person understands ADHD issues. If he or she doesn't, the professional could contribute to playing the blame game rather than help the two of you move away from it.

Pattern 7 Walking on Eggshells, Anger Spurts, and Rude Behavior

If you are a non-ADHD spouse, you probably have the feeling that you are walking on eggshells, not knowing what might come next. Will your spouse unexpectedly blow up or stomp off? Will he forget to do something he promised to do? Will he interrupt you often or say things that are so "truthful," they hurt?

These tantrums, spurts of anger, and rude behaviors often accompany ADHD and have to do with lack of impulse control and the emotional dysregulation that comes with ADHD. As this plays out in your relationship, the result is that a non-ADHD spouse feels as if she can never relax. She feels she must always be wary and vigilant.

ADHD spouses may also feel as if they are walking on eggshells. One man with ADHD described it to me as "having to anticipate my wife's response to every single thing I do. I live my life trying to second guess her because I want to please her, but most of the time she's just mad!"

It's obvious that behaviors described in the first paragraph are the result of ADHD symptoms, which should be treated to lessen their impact on your relationship. It's less obvious, but no less true, that the anger a non-ADHD spouse expresses is also often a symptom of having ADHD in your relationship. Thinking of anger this way helps both partners depersonalize it and create a specific plan to "treat" it.

You'll find much more information about this in Step 2.

Pattern 8 Pursuit and Escape

Very frequently, ADHD couples get into a situation where a non-ADHD spouse aggressively pursues the ADHD spouse by nagging, escalating the emotional content of conversations, and sometimes physically following a spouse around. This is done in an effort to get the ADHD spouse to "pay attention," do things, and *change*. Pursuit happens because without it, the non-ADHD spouse gets ignored (ADHD symptom: distraction). It's also part survival strategy. If things don't change, marriage for the non-ADHD partner will continue to be painful, and eventually become untenable. She feels she has no choice but to become more aggressive (or to disconnect completely, which is a different approach not considered in this section).

Many times, the non-ADHD spouse's pursuit is done with the best of intentions:

> My husband and I got married relatively young (25) and we have been married for almost four years. Before we got married, I guess I knew that he had ADD but it didn't seem like a big deal. He had a decent job and an apartment and money in the bank. He paid his bills and shopped for groceries and cooked his own food. But after we got married he started to go downhill.... He has no self-control or ability to make himself work. Especially when I'm not hovering nearby to make sure he's working.... I guess my big problem is that he never seems to try to make any real changes. He says he tries, but that his brain is broken. I understand that it's a LOT harder for him than the average person, but in my opinion he hasn't yet given it his all. He stopped taking his depression meds because they were making him groggy (didn't discuss this with his dr.), rarely takes his Adderall because sometimes it doesn't work (I don't get this!)....
>
> I feel like I have begged, pleaded, cried, yelled to get his attention but it never works...or never works for long. If I get mad, I'm the bad guy because I'm not supportive. If I get sad it makes him feel worse about himself. Basically I feel like there is nothing more I can do. I've tried so hard to help him: finding therapists for him, buying him books...printing out articles about tips, coping strategies, etc. for dealing with ADD, checking in to make sure he's doing his projects (he never is),

> encouraging him to exercise with me, take his meds, etc. Honestly, he should've been doing many of these things for himself, but he didn't, so I did. It's pretty much the way our relationship works—he doesn't do what he is supposed to do so I swoop in and try to keep things from falling apart.
>
> I'm sick of it. I want an equal (ok, halfway equal?) partner. At some point, I have to cut my losses and move on if he isn't capable of making any changes. I'm not asking for a perfect husband [but I] feel like I've given so much and tried so hard to help him and it hasn't made any difference at all. This relationship has taken so much out of me and the return just does not seem worth it some days.

This woman has tried and tried *and tried* to get her husband to manage his own ADHD. Yet she remains frustrated by his "retreat" from her efforts.

Fearing failure once again, an ADHD spouse will likely "escape" into one of three responses:

1. Acquiescence, but with a high likelihood that he won't follow through because of ADHD symptoms
2. Anger and defensiveness, a shame response that effectively delays the conversation
3. Denial or avoidance (the most obvious form of escape)

The husband in the quote above is doing both the first and the last.

Another common form of escape is to become too busy with other things to be responsive. In my family, that meant lots of computer time for my husband. After our relationship declined, he would come home from work and make a beeline for his office and computer, not to be seen again (except to eat) until after I was asleep.

As you can imagine, "escape" doesn't sit well with any non-ADHD spouse who thinks her requests are reasonable and doesn't understand why her spouse is so unwilling to simply be responsible or responsive. She personalizes his retreat, figuring that his lack of desire to help out is rooted in a basic lack of respect for her, her needs, and their partnership, rather than the result of shame, fear, or hopelessness. ("If he *really* cared, he would try harder.")

His retreat also places a heavy burden on her. It's one thing to do more than your share or be lonely for a short period of time...but forever? As with the couple above, repeated retreat causes a non-ADHD spouse to lose hope that she will ever get a break, while her increasingly desperate pursuit and agitation causes him greater and greater anxiety. Escape seems a reasonable path.

This is a perfect example where knowing more about ADHD in the relationship can change a pattern. To address this spiral, this husband could acknowledge that his ADHD symptoms are causing problems for his wife, and treat them *effectively* in order to change the pattern. That means doing things he already knows that he should do: take his medications regularly, work with his doctor to find the medication that helps him, and find a cognitive behavioral therapist or ADHD coach to help him change his behaviors around the home. He's "in control" here because he's the one with the symptoms, no matter how hard she tries.

She could take some of the "pursuer" pressure off her spouse by choosing to assist him in a very few well-defined areas that are particularly important to her own well-being. She might also want to work with a marriage counselor to start discovering ways to satisfy her own emotional needs so she is less involved with his every move (and failure). Given their ages and her feelings about the marriage, she should let him know that she will not remain in the marriage unless he takes more responsibility for mitigating his ADHD symptoms. He showed her he could do it before their marriage; he should be able to do it again. Perhaps a marriage counselor can help the two of them identify whether any part of their interactions is hampering his efforts.

Tips
Dealing with Pursuit and Escape

- **Aggressive pursuit, even when offered as "help," can paralyze an ADHD partner**, who may well see it as one of a long series of comments on his or her competence. If the ADHD spouse is in retreat, pursuit may be playing a role.

- **Pursuit often signals desperation**. If you are an ADHD spouse, understand that aggressive pursuit is often an indication of *desperation* in your spouse, not a sign that your previously mild-mannered partner has become a control freak. Look for ADHD's impact. See a therapist or doctor to try to get at the root issues of the non-ADHD spouse's desperation, and figure out which symptoms need more attention in your treatment.

Pattern 9
Nag Now, Pay Later

One form of pursuit is nagging, and if you are a non-ADHD spouse, I am guessing you do it.

Perhaps five years into my marriage, my mother, who normally refrained from commenting on my marriage, went so far as to take me aside and tell me that I needed to leave my husband be. I was after him all the time, she told me, and that would be bad for my marriage.

My response at the time was to tell her that I felt I *had* to nag him; otherwise, I would be completely stranded with two small children to take care of. I felt as if I was fighting for my life. When I "went after him," I was seeking any scraps of attention, respect, help, and support I could get. He was so distant from me that the only way I could get his attention was to be right in his face.

There are few unhappy non-ADHD wives who don't nag their spouses–a lot–to pay attention to them and to do things differently. You may think you don't nag. If this is the case, ask your partner. (Non-ADHD men "nag" their ADHD wives, too, but it comes out differently—as domination.) Often, the non-ADHD spouse feels the nagging is justified, just as I did. Her husband's lack of attention or inability to follow through has driven her to it. (The blame game again!)

I am here to tell you, having been there, that it is time to take control of yourself and choose to go in a different direction. Although it may seem counterintuitive, a nagging spouse will be much more successful if she stops nagging completely and follows the ideas in this book. Nagging puts your entire relationship at risk by changing the proportion of positive interactions to negative interactions heavily in favor of the negative.

The most important reason not to nag is that it's completely and totally ineffective over the long term. Since the underlying issue is the ADHD partner's distractibility and untreated ADHD, rather than motivation, nagging is not an effective tool for getting things done. Treatment is.

There are lots of other reasons not to nag:

- It exacerbates the desire of the ADHD partner to retreat from the non-ADHD partner, increasing loneliness and separation.
- It most often moves the relationship into the destructive parent–child pattern.
- It reinforces the shame that the ADHD partner feels, because it reminds him of many shame-filled times from his past when he was also nagged to do something by teachers or parents.
- Because of the pervasiveness of the distractibility of the ADHD partner, nagging in ADHD relationships becomes a way of life, rather than an occasional event. The result is that it changes each partner's self-image for the worse. One starts to think he's no good since there's so much nagging, and the other starts to dislike herself because she's become a witch.

In non-ADHD relationships, you can get away with some occasional nagging because the nagging is directed toward fixing a different problem: that of a temporary lack of motivation. In ADHD-affected relationships, you simply can't get away with nagging, because nagging doesn't effectively address the underlying issue: an ADHD symptom.

To put it another way, nagging as a method of addressing the ADHD symptom of distractibility is like hitting your head against a wall over and over again until you are *both* exhausted. It's time to stop nagging and develop a more positive and *much* more effective approach that gets to the heart of the real issue: treating ADHD and taking it into account as you interact. If you cannot make this change, you will quite possibly end up divorced.

Tips
Stop Nagging

- **Just say "no."** Nagging is a choice. There are other ways to express your needs, as well as to ensure that a partner who has trouble remembering things gets them done. Listen to yourself to learn to keep your words in check, and this will become a healthier habit than speaking reflexively.
- **Agree to specific language to point out nagging as it happens**. Seeing just how often it's happening is likely to make you want to do it less. A phrase like "Would you modify your request, please? That sounds like nagging to me," can work.
- **Treat the underlying ADHD symptoms** that are causing the friction leading to nagging (there are more resources about treatment later in the book). Usually the symptoms that lead to nagging are distraction and difficulty initiating tasks. Treatment for these symptoms includes physical changes such as medication, which can improve brain focus, and behavioral changes such as developing organizational or reminder systems that get you going at the right time.

Pattern 10
Losing Faith in Your Spouse and Yourself

One of the saddest patterns that develops in ADHD-affected marriages is when both partners lose faith in themselves and each other. Before she got married, the ADHD spouse thought she had found someone who accepted her for who she is and who would help her to make her sometimes very difficult life a bit easier. Instead, she ended up with a partner for whom she is never good enough and who wants her to change. She is told, verbally or nonverbally, that she is unreliable and worthless. The one thing she is certain of is that sometime in the not-too-distant future, she will have to endure her spouse's anger, frustration, scorn, or rejection for something she did "wrong." What had promised to be a supportive and caring relationship now distorts how she feels about herself:

> I have ADD and Anxiety. Before I married, I did have a hard time in school and some minor things like a cluttered house but not dirty…I was pretty happy-go-lucky, I had friends who loved me for me, my family loved me very much. I loved me very much. I was spontaneous but not reckless; I had my art and a nice little job at a gallery. I was eclectic and funny and…happy.
>
> I met my husband and he seemed to love me for me. He claimed he didn't mind my cluttered house and that he loved how outspoken and zany I was. We lived together for three years before we got married, and after the wedding it seemed I had started to wear on him, he developed true resentment [towards] me for these behaviors and "ways" that he used to say he loved so much.
>
> "Why do you do this?" he would ask, and I honestly couldn't tell him. It was how I always did things, it was how we did things while we were dating and living together. He started to complain about me behind my back, telling his mother and my family how lazy I was, how he hated how outspoken I was, how he wanted the house to look like a Martha Stewart home like his mom's house.
>
> He resents me for being me, basically. I resent him for resenting me! We love each other, but this is getting to be too much. The things he used to love he now hates. He hates me! He used to tell me to never change and now he wants me to change for him!

> So, on top of the ADD, now I feel anxious, and well, honestly, depressed. I will never be FIXED, and it feels hopeless. I love my husband, but his anger/resentment for how I operate is starting to take a toll on me. I hate me now! I have no friends now, my family hates me now because of all the bad things he tells them about me. He complains all the time. A cup of coffee on the counter is evil!
>
> I drive my husband nuts with my forgetfulness, even though I never forget super-important stuff, just little stuff, like buying milk on the way home. I don't forget things on purpose and I take care of important things. My life is always spinning out of control. It never did before! I have been in argument after argument with my husband, he yells all the time. He yells because my blouse is wrinkled.
>
> I do my best, and I sat him down and told him that. I told him I'm doing what I can and working my hardest but there is only so much I can do without his help. He tells me to grow up and put out towels that match....
>
> I feel like I'm being pulled in a million different directions and it's so overwhelming. I feel worthless!... I've been completely and utterly drowning this year, and working a lot more with very little help from my husband. I try and put on a brave face and struggle through. It's unbearable sometimes...
>
> He tells me [it's] all my problem and he won't help, he just works and comes home and yells because the floor is dirty at the door and the laundry isn't folded yet. He calls me terrible names in front of the kids and calls me names to our families. Like lazy, stupid....

This woman wants to be accepted for who she is. Sadly, the ADHD symptoms she has always had are now getting the best of her life. She has two children, which has put a premium on organization in the household. It seems as if her husband is trying to "bring her into line" by raising (or perhaps enforcing) certain household standards he didn't used to worry about and has developed anger and resentment issues that may require professional help. This pattern is common. By raising the household standards he is, in essence, insisting that she become "non-ADHD." A much better approach would be to accept her and her ADHD and figure out how to *get around* remaining ADHD symptoms that her treatment hasn't helped. A housekeeper and organizer could go a long way toward making this household function better if the non-ADHD husband were willing to call a truce, and a counselor could help the two of them work through the emotional damage already inflicted.

It's not just the ADHD spouse who loses faith in herself. I remember feeling as if I didn't like myself anymore after years of being held hostage by the anger, frustration, and stress of being married to an untreated ADHD spouse. I had turned into a mean, bitter woman I no longer recognized. It was a huge turning point for me when I decided to take control of who I was once again and start living life as the person I really wanted to be instead of as a victim of ADHD.

It is when you start to lose faith in each other that you start to question why you got married in the first place and whether you can survive as a couple. Your negative view of today colors what you remember from yesterday. Recently, a non-ADHD woman said to her spouse while I was listening: "I don't trust you now, and I don't think I have ever trusted you in the past, and I feel confident that I'll never trust you in the future." Is that statement *really* likely to be true? She did marry him, after all, and presumably she trusted him enough to decide to join lives together. Yet she has become so entangled in the bad feelings, so sad, so angry, so different from what she thought she could be, that divorce starts to look like an appealing solution. But it is not the only way out.

The overwhelming feelings you are having about each other are a result of dealing with ADHD symptoms. In other words, though the feelings are real, the underlying causes of the feelings are "treatable" with the right approach. It will take time to rebuild your trust in each other, but it most certainly can be done. You are, at your most basic foundations, the same people you were when you married. You are simply interacting differently due to the unexpected and, until now, invisible pressures of the *ADHD effect* in your relationship.

Most couples will not return to the giddiness that they felt during courtship. This has nothing to do with ADHD or your experiences, but with the chemicals that are released by infatuation. Researcher Helen Fisher, who studies the chemistry of love, knows that romantic love and infatuation creates and is fueled by, among other things, unusually high levels of dopamine. The giddy, romantic part of a relationship—of all relationships, not just yours—"mellows" when dopamine levels return to more normal levels. This happens to almost all couples.

The good news is that you can find something *better* than that giddiness, something that you value because it is deep and real and based on an appreciation for who you are, warts and all, not just on chemicals that are released when you first get to know each other.

Tips

Not Losing Faith

- **Blame the ADHD symptoms**, not yourself. Then set out to make the changes necessary to conquer them.
- **Think about who you want to be in your life**. Many of the choices we make day to day are just that—choices. Set up a positive framework for yourself that helps you make choices you feel good about. This will go a long way toward preventing you from losing faith in yourself. I describe this process in detail in Step 5.
- **Get support**. Find a support group, a therapist, some friends, family. Don't work through your bad feelings about yourself alone. Let them help you focus on the positive and on changing your future.

Pattern 11
Your Sexual Relationship Breaks Down

As the ADHD-affected relationship breaks down, sex becomes strained or nonexistent. The key reasons for this change include many factors:

- Anger, frustration, sadness, verbal abuse, and parent–child relationships ruin the desire for intimacy.
- People with ADHD often take their distraction to bed. Without meaning to, they can communicate "I'm not interested" to their partner as their mind wanders in a different direction, or as sex takes less and less time.
- Distracted ADHD partners can be hard to get into bed in the first place. Scheduled sex may not seem romantic to partners, resulting in less sex. Non-ADHD partners frequently misinterpret this symptom, and start to think that their partner isn't interested in them anymore.
- Conversely, non-ADHD spouses can become very resentful if their normally distracted husband who seems to pay them no attention suddenly hones in on them for sex (but can't be bothered to carry his weight around the house at any other time). Sex becomes just another chore.
- Sex can become a tool to control a spouse. "Behave a certain way or I won't have sex with you" becomes one form of punishment for perceived incompetency in other areas or anger.
- Particularly difficult relationships can lead to either emotional or physical infidelity, as one spouse or the other seeks escape from the unrelenting stresses of the marriage.
- People with ADHD have a tendency toward addictive behaviors, including pornography, affairs, and impulsive sexual actions. Discovery of this can put the brakes on a couple's sexual relationship.

- As the ability to communicate breaks down, the ability to recover or laugh at sexual mishaps lessens, meaning that every risk or change taken in a sexual relationship becomes a possible vehicle for failure. Couples tend to retreat, and sex can become stale (which bores and saddens them both) or be eliminated all together.

If this seems like a particularly gloomy picture, it is. However, it is fixable. My personal philosophy is that the underlying issues—ADHD symptoms, anger, and miscommunication—need to be addressed before a couple's sexual relationship can return to full health. The good news is that the "living in the moment" aspect of the ADHD spouse can be used to help speed that repair once basic issues are resolved. I include a section on bringing the fun and romance back into your sex life later in the book.

Tips

Handling It When Sex Becomes a Problem

- **Don't force it.** Returning your sexual relationship to health will be one of the last things you do, since it's deeply intertwined with other aspects of your relationship.
- **Build intimacy in other ways**. Hold hands, go for walks together, spend cuddle time together in the morning or evening without sex, talk to each other about your dreams for the future.
- **Schedule intimate time**. If distraction is the issue, schedule times to have sex together and try some new techniques. Vary locations and positions, try to be spontaneous, experiment with sex toys, share erotic fiction and sex fantasies. While you're scheduling sex, consider scheduling foreplay, too.
- **Consider medication or exercise**. Treatment can improve focus at specific times, including for sex. Short-acting medication or scheduling sex after exercising can help banish distraction.
- **Get counseling** for pornography or sex addictions. Make sure to use someone who understands ADHD.

Pattern 12
Believing ADHD Doesn't Matter

Even after all of the patterns I've laid out, some ADHD spouses still won't believe that ADHD is a factor in *their* relationship. This can be a real source of friction.

I've lived this dilemma, for my husband blamed me for years for our issues. When I suggested he get treatment for his ADHD, his angry response was "I don't need treatment! I like myself FINE just the way I am. YOU'RE the one who doesn't like me and has issues in this relationship!" I will tell you that this particular denial response, if you hear it, is one of the most frustrating parts of living with an ADHD spouse.

The good news for us was that about a month or so after diagnosis my husband decided that even though he wasn't completely comfortable and still thought I was the villain, he didn't have much to lose by considering treatment. He figured that even if treatment didn't do anything, trying something new would at least improve his chances that I would "get off his back."

So this is my plea to all of you ADHD partners who are still skeptical: **Even if you don't *believe* ADHD matters, I'm going to ask you to *assume* that it matters, and get the full evaluation and pursue effective treatment**. Here's why this is the best course of action:

- There's no downside to seeing what a well thought out treatment might do for your relationship, but there is a potentially huge upside. Remember, treatment doesn't have to include medication.

- Most of the anger and problems in the non-ADHD spouse right now are really and truly a reflection of dealing with ADHD symptoms. Think of it as a black hole. You can't see the center of it (the ADHD), but you know it's there, because there's so much commotion around its edges. If the patterns of this chapter are in your relationship, then the chances are very good that ADHD is not being adequately dealt with.

- Non-ADHD spouses whose ADHD partners assume responsibility for their ADHD are *much* more likely to calm down a bit and admit that yes, they too play a big role in their marriage problems. Wouldn't it be nicer to live with a person who is working on her own issues, too, rather than just being angry at you all the time?
- Since they are biologically based, denying that ADHD issues exist doesn't make them go away. The only thing denial does is exacerbate the issues by making those around you miserable.
- If you try to treat ADHD—and by this, I mean really go after it, not just make one pass at taking medication—you will be in no worse a place than you currently find yourself. If you don't like the results or if medication doesn't work for you, you can try something else, or even return to what you are doing (or not doing) now. But millions *do* like the results and see their lives change dramatically for the better.
- If you don't make the leap of faith and assume that ADHD is a factor, then the statistics suggest that your marriage will, more likely than not, become dysfunctional and very possibly end in divorce. Wouldn't it be worth it just to see what *might* happen?

Remember, you are the only person who can take charge of the impact that ADHD has on your relationship. If you worry your attempts will fail, I would like to challenge your thinking. In the past, you haven't known which tools might help you. This book and other resources I'll point out can change that.

I know that you already do a lot of things in your life to accommodate ADHD, so I'm not asking you to *try harder*. I'm asking you to *try differently*. I'm not asking you to change yourself. I'm asking you to address symptoms so that the real you—that wonderful person who is suffering unnecessarily because of the impact of a biological difference—shines through. You may think your wife or husband wants to change you. They may even say that. But what they *really* want is for the real you—the warm, caring, crazy, energetic, happy, perhaps even zany person they fell in love with—to come back without so much of the symptom "baggage." They want to be able to love you unreservedly, without having to make so many of the horrific tradeoffs in their own lives that responding to your symptoms requires.

Will it be easy? No. Is there a magic pill? No. Is it worth the effort? More than I can possibly convey.

Still not sure? Read the words of four people with ADHD who did not initially think their ADHD had an impact on their lives or marriages:

> I was quite resistant to taking meds (I just generally don't take much of anything, and I tend to need a kid's dose when I do) but one of the big surprises when I finally tried them was that social situations just plain got easier. I hadn't realized quite how much energy they took before, only that I didn't much like those kinds of casual large-group scenes where you know lots of people but not all that well and you can't sit down and have a real conversation...I take a kid-sized dose of Adderall and in addition to being able to be on time most of the time (without having to plan every minute and focus on nothing but being on time) I find that those "social hour" situations have gotten WAY easier.... I have found that [meds] give me a new paradigm—a new framework—for understanding how I navigate the world.

> I was just diagnosed with ADD and OCD. I didn't really expect the OCD, however my list of 32+ concerns may have put me over the top....[In my life] everything always got done, however I always felt like I was scattered on 80 projects, not organized (with infinite lists), and worried.
>
> I recently started meds to address some of the

issues. WITHOUT HESITATION, I feel like I've had the best week of my life...my worrying has reduced, I have been so much more productive, I can't seem to get the tape recorder to turn on in my brain (I keep waiting), and so much more.

Initially, I didn't like having a label/diagnosis. I felt like I really should be able to be fabulous with all of my success and will-power on my own. Now, I wonder how much time I've wasted over the years. I feel very much like my brain was in overdrive—always. I was exhausted —always. I'm still learning a lot. I definitely, though, have a new appreciation for my world.

This post is...addressed to [Tom and to] all the ADHD spouses who still remain clueless about the impacts of the ADHD on their relationships, and are inadvertently driving their spouses to leave them. Tom is confused by his wife's leaving because he asserts he is a good person and thought the marriage was good.

To Tom:

Where your instincts may fail you is how your ADHD-influenced actions affect other people around you, especially your spouse. My first marriage ended after five years. To me, everything seemed fine, and then one day she just left. For many years I was puzzled as to why she left, and always thought it was her fault (as did most of our friends).

Only now, in retrospect, do I understand why she may have left. That retrospection came from a twenty year second marriage that went right to the brink, with my believing that I was OK, a good husband, and the issues were with my wife. It did not end in divorce, ONLY because I began to realize how my actions (or non-actions) negatively affected my wife. Surprisingly, the road to that discovery and the self-awareness came from working for a boss who had a very bad case of ADHD (the case for many entrepreneurs and CEOs). Seeing my actions in a mirror came as quite a shock.

Things like outbursts of anger or harsh responses, that most ADHD don't even realize they do, have an incredible impact on those with whom they have a relationship...so ditch your "instincts." You really cannot begin to comprehend how your actions affect others. You may not be bad, but your actions have a very significant negative impact on those you love.

Second, understand the difference between a "bad person" and one whose however inadvertent actions negatively impact others. If you cling to your instincts and your worldview of equating good motives with good outcome, you will fail.

I'm a man in my early 40s, married 12 years, have two wonderful young boys (elementary school age) with my wife. After the last several years of anger, frustration of why we're both not happy, our marriage counselor finally got around to asking me something: Dan, do you think you have ADD? So after the usual procrastination a couple more months, I finally saw a psychologist. I have just been diagnosed in the last couple weeks that I have ADHD and I'm now taking Strattera, so far just 1 week...but it's about 1 month too late, as my wife and I are now separated and planning to divorce. Divorce is the consequence of ADHD...left undetected for years.

It's unfortunate...[when] husbands either don't accept they have ADD/ADHD or know they have it yet still don't want to get therapy or take medications. Frankly, these married men simply need to be slapped upside their heads by another married man that also has

ADHD and does accept and has seen its effects. Divorce is awful for two people who loved each other, got married and had wonderful children, but broke apart over the years because of ADHD....

I believe the true character of a man...any married man with ADD/ADHD...is shown when he doesn't fight his spouse, but he fights his ADD/ADHD. It's not courageous to fight a loving, generous woman, it's very courageous to fight a powerful, sneaky, and vicious ADHD within oneself. Like myself, perhaps some men need to be figuratively slapped upside the head before they finally get it.

Rebuilding Your Relationship in Six Steps

Six Steps to a Better Relationship

"Delay is the deadliest form of denial."
—Proverb

In your eagerness and desperation, you might have skipped right to this section, ignoring the first part of the book. That's understandable, but when you're done reading this section, go back to read the first part. If you're going to address ADHD in your marriage, you need to know how it presents itself. Being able to say, "That's ADHD at work, and I'm going to step away from it" is an important weapon in your arsenal.

Why six steps? The problems you are facing are complex and ingrained. The steps provide a road map to help you sort it all out and make your journey.

With each step you will gain insight into your mutual problems, as well as ideas about how to address them. Offering a variety of targeted ideas acknowledges the presence of ADHD. Although it's true that many patterns exist, ADHD manifests itself uniquely in each individual (and that's one reason it is so hard to treat and manage). So yours will be a journey of experimentation, in much the same way that ADHD treatment is experimentation, until you find a series of systems that reasonably accommodate ADHD while satisfying both partners. An idea will resonate with you, and you'll try it and measure its success. Did it work? If so, keep it and make it part of your lives. If not, try another idea under the same theme.

The ideas I'm presenting have worked for others in your situation. And they are presented in the order that I have found to be the most effective in changing marriages for the better.

Some of these ideas may seem simple, but to implement them can take a radical shift in your thinking and behavior. For example, I challenge you to banish harsh words and find constructive outlets for anger. I urge ADHD spouses to try a specific approach to treatment. I ask you to set up boundaries and structures in your relationship that don't currently exist.

Why? Because right now, what you are doing is not working. Nibbling at ADHD issues around the edges of your relationship by making small changes isn't going to work, either. ADHD is bigger than that. You can let it ruin your relationship, or you can take control in this fight. Because this is a fight. You don't have to be victims of ADHD; together, you and your spouse can take control so you can thrive and become, once again, the partners you had hoped to be.

Step 1: Cultivating Empathy for Your Spouse

"Although we all agree in principle that our partners have their own points of view and their own valid perceptions, at the emotional level we are reluctant to accept this simple truth."
— Harville Hendrix, *Getting the Love You Want*

You and your spouse are much more different than you realize.

If you have ADHD, I *guarantee* that you underestimate the impact your ADHD has on your non-ADHD spouse. Your symptoms have transformed your partner's life. It's important for you to understand what that transformation feels and looks like so you can better understand your spouse's behavior.

If you are the non-ADHD spouse, gaining a deeper insight into and respect for your spouse's everyday struggles is necessary in order to change your own behaviors in a way that will lead you toward a more harmonious relationship. Until you can summon this empathy, you risk falling into one of the darker traps of an ADHD relationship: assuming that your way of doing things is superior to that of the ADHD spouse.

A non-ADHD spouse doesn't have to say this aloud. All she has to do is insist that things be done her way, not his. Yes, she may be more efficient, but that is not the only dimension of a relationship; in fact, I would argue that in the long run it is a relatively unimportant dimension of a relationship, except when you are both working and have small children relying on you. Then, efficiency can be a significant benefit in ensuring the safety of your children. Examples of this might include purchasing and installing a baby gate before a newly walking child falls down the stairs, or getting kids to bed at a reasonable hour so that they are alert and less prone to accidents.

Before further exploring the experiences of each spouse, I would like to remind you that these observations were written by people in crisis. They are struggling in their marriages, and this struggle has affected how they are able to cope in the world. Sometimes crisis brings out characteristics that are normally held at bay. A common example would be the behavior of an ADHD spouse who becomes paralyzed by fear of disappointing her spouse (or of angering him) if she tries and fails. This might not have been a factor earlier in their relationship, but now the stress of their daily interactions has affected her ability to cope. Because I focus on the aspects of each spouse's experiences that are relevant to understand while you are in crisis, I leave out the parts that make each of you so wonderful and uniquely great to be with.

The couples in these examples are in crisis, and the pictures that they paint are sobering, even bleak. However, their desperation does not indicate that there is no hope for them as couples, but rather that they have not been addressing their issues in ways that are appropriate for couples struggling with ADHD. In fact, many of the things they have tried up to this point are the opposite of what works with ADHD. Understand that ADHD in your relationship does not in any way doom you to a bleak existence or hopeless situation. (Nor does living with a partner with "attention surplus disorder," as Ned Hallowell jokingly calls those of us who don't have ADHD!) Both of you have within you the ability to live joyous, loving, companionable lives filled with happiness.

The experiences of both spouses fall within a spectrum. Some non-ADHD partners are confused and annoyed by their spouse's behavior, but not yet into the phase that includes crippling anger or hopelessness. Some ADHD spouses have relatively minor symptoms or have had good success getting their symptoms under control. They may not suffer from feeling overwhelmed or feeling as if they must hide their ADHD.

Some experiences might surprise you as they go "unvoiced" in daily life. It is my hope that these descriptions will open up deeper conversations about what it's like to be each of you while you are in crisis, and help you better understand your partner's actions.

First we'll consider a quick overview of important concepts for the ADHD spouse's experience, and then read the words of those who live these experiences every day, taken primarily from the ADHD and marriage blog found at www.adhdmarriage.com.

What It's Like to Be an ADHD Spouse in Marital Crisis

There is a spectrum of ADHD symptoms. Some people, like my husband, have no trouble with ADHD in one or more realms (such as work), yet suffer in another (close relationships). Those with the most severe symptoms find that ADHD interferes with just about everything. In either case, in those realms of life in which ADHD plays a role, a person with ADHD often experiences the following feelings:

- **Different.** The brain is often racing, and people with ADHD experience the world in a way that others don't easily understand or relate to.
- **Overwhelmed, secretly or overtly**. Keeping daily life under control takes *much* more work than others realize.
- **Subordinate to their spouses**. Their partners spend a good deal of time correcting them or running the show. The corrections make them feel incompetent, and often contribute to a parent–child dynamic. Men can describe these interactions as making them feel emasculated.
- **Shamed**. They often hide a large amount of shame, sometimes compensating with bluster or retreat.
- **Unloved and unwanted**. Consistent reminders from spouses, bosses, and others that they should "change" reinforce that they are unloved as they are.

- **Afraid to fail again.** As their relationships worsen, the potential of punishment for failure increases. But ADHD inconsistency means this partner *will* fail at some point. Anticipating this failure results in reluctance to try.
- **Longing to be accepted.** One of the strongest emotional desires of those with ADHD is to be loved as they are, in spite of imperfections.
- **Relieved.** When treatment helps and they can start to take control of their lives again, few want to "go back."

The best way to find out what having ADHD is like is to listen to those who experience it. Many talk about disorganization, noise, or buzz in their heads. Dr. Ned Hallowell describes it this way:[8]

> It's like listening to a radio station with a lot of static and you have to strain to hear what's going on. Or, it's like trying to build a house of cards in a dust storm. You have to build a structure to protect yourself from the wind before you can even start on the cards.
>
> In other ways it's like being super-charged all the time. You get one idea and you have to act on it, and then, what do you know, but you've got another idea before you've finished up with the first one, and so you go for that one, but of course a third idea intercepts the second, and you just have to follow that one, and pretty soon people are calling you disorganized and impulsive and all sorts of impolite words that miss the point completely. Because you're trying really hard. It's just that you have all these invisible vectors pulling you this way and that which makes it really hard to stay on task.
>
> Plus which, you're spilling over all the time. You're drumming your fingers, tapping your feet, humming a song, whistling, looking here, looking there, scratching, stretching, doodling, and people think you're not paying

8. Hallowell, Edward M., *What's It Like to Have ADD?*, © 1992. Used with permission of author.

> attention or that you're not interested, but all you're doing is spilling over so that you can pay attention. I can pay a lot better attention when I'm taking a walk or listening to music or even when I'm in a crowded, noisy room than when I'm still and surrounded by silence…
>
> What is it like to have ADHD? Buzzing. Being here and there and everywhere. Someone once said, "Time is the thing that keeps everything from happening all at once." Time parcels moments out into separate bits so that we can do one thing at a time. In ADHD, this does not happen. In ADHD, time collapses. Time becomes a black hole. To the person with ADHD it feels as if everything is happening all at once. This creates a sense of inner turmoil or even panic. The individual loses perspective and the ability to prioritize. He or she is always on the go, trying to keep the world from caving in on top.

Hallowell describes the physical feeling of ADHD beautifully—the buzzing, crowding, doodling, spilling over, out-of-control activity that can be a part of everyday life for a person with ADHD. But there is an emotional side as well, and it is often darker than "spilling over" might suggest. Hidden shame and fear of failure plague most who have suffered long periods of undiagnosed ADHD. (I would like to point out here that people who have managed their ADHD since childhood and grown up with it as only one part of their personality do much better in this area.) This man with ADHD has written a wonderful description of the shame he has experienced:

> I was not diagnosed with ADD until I was 33 years old …[ADHD] affected my self perception [similar to] how an anorexic feels fat or overweight when looking in the mirror even as they waste away and are emaciated. For me I have a low self esteem or sense of self worth no matter if I am a huge success or a failure. I never could congratulate myself because if am responsible for my success then I must also be to blame for my failures.

When I was diagnosed at 33 yrs old and I learned I have a brain problem not a motivation or stupidity problem, I was elated for about a month. I read everything I could find to better understand it [and] I began to realize my years of trying to overcome my limitations by just trying harder and increasing my efforts to just trying to pretend I was normal or okay, or even mediocre was the wrong approach. I needed to admit that my effort and motivation was not the cause of my problems like disorganization, procrastination etc. and until I developed new skills with the help of medication that I could only put forth an illusion of control.

The illusion I worked to maintain was that I was normal…but inside deep down I ALWAYS KNEW IT WAS A LIE. I hid my shame…I knew I was a "no good lazy stupid person" even if others didn't always agree. I wasn't afraid of work so much as being judged for the results because I never knew if I would produce a good or bad outcome or how I ended up with one or the other. After I learned of my ADD I knew I would sometimes backslide, fail to consistently get results I wanted. Many times I still feel like giving up, or just saying I can't do it! I quit!…running away and hiding is easier than to admit my unworthiness to the world.

Some days it is a struggle to keep my life together even in the little ways most people take for granted. After all, if I can't make sure my socks make it into a hamper how is it I can take care of a seriously ill patient in an emergency? A four year old can be taught to put their clothes away but I can't? The past 30 years of my life I either heard from my parents, teachers, coaches, peers, coworkers, managers, brother, girlfriends that I could be so much more if only I tried harder or worked harder…. So it taught me to hate myself and to develop a kit of behaviors and adaptations for basic survival.

> I became an expert at making it look like I knew what I was doing, I learned to lie to cover for mistakes, or missed assignments or poor performance, I learned to deflect criticism to shift the blame to anything or anyone other than myself to protect my fragile ego. When that didn't work and my ego was still threatened I sometimes blew up—made a scene one minute and was completely calm the next moment. I also learned to sabotage. I earned a PhD in Excuse Making and a Masters Degree in Apologies. I could also act like the wounded animal and elicit other people's need to provide help to get me out of doing it for myself. These all are unhealthy but totally understandable behaviors and adaptations to a wounded sense of self worth.
>
> Once I learned of my ADD these habits and feelings didn't disappear, but my excuses I gave began to sound hollow. I realized now I had other options because I knew what the problem was. I could change the outcomes not by necessarily working harder but by working differently.
>
> So now I try to not avoid uncomfortable conflicts, to not need to always be the peacemaker, and I try to be more decisive—not to just defer the decisions so someone else can take the blame. I still fight my urges to withdraw into myself or seek distractions in mindless and meaningless activity whether surfing the internet or walking Walmart aisles for 2-3 hours in the middle of the night, or losing myself in a bookstore for 10 hours instead of dealing with whatever I am avoiding that day. I still do these things but I try and set a time limit. I still can frustrate my wife taking two hours to get gas for my car.

This man has started to confront his ADHD and his hidden shame, putting into place strategies like setting time limits and being more decisive about what he needs. These strategies will help him begin to overcome those ADHD symptoms that are hurting him most.

But think about these words again: "I wasn't afraid of work so much as being judged for the results because I never knew if I would produce a good or bad outcome or how I ended up with one or the other." Here's another quote that voices a similar idea: "Even when I manage to do something right I tend to write it off. I view it more as an accident than anything else."

Imagine the stress of living your life knowing that you could never be confident that hard work would result in a good outcome! This reality of untreated ADHD is quite different from what most non-ADHD spouses have experienced, and it goes a long way toward explaining the ambivalence of so many ADHD adults when it comes to taking on difficult challenges. Good treatment works, in part, because it improves consistency in the life of a person with ADHD. Sometimes for the first time in his life, a person with ADHD can be fairly assured that the treatment and coping strategies he has put in place will mean that hard work will produce a desirable outcome and not blow up in his face.

Non-ADHD spouses frequently tell me that they are intensely frustrated that their spouses don't "take ADHD more seriously and do something about it." They view this as a lack of will or strength. Yet what I observe is that fear, or the coping strategy of retreat, often motivates their paralysis. They've created a precarious life balance that lets them "get along" in the world. But it might come tumbling down if disturbed too much, and so far most of the coping strategies they have in place are not optimal. Is this frustrating to the non-ADHD spouse? Of course! The *logical* choice, *if you are used to being successful when you attempt something difficult,* would be to address the symptoms and change your future for the better. But in the untreated ADHD life, one "logical" choice might be to not try and therefore not risk failure. When the stakes get higher, as they do when your marriage is disintegrating, "not trying" becomes increasingly appealing because the potential results of failure, including divorce, become so devastating.

While a good proportion of people, particularly men with ADHD, report they feel vulnerable to being "found out," virtually all of those with ADHD who are currently having marital issues feel unloved. They generally feel they are "different," and long to be accepted and loved for who they are. This is not unique to the ADHD spouse, of course, but what may surprise you is that as miserable as you know the non-ADHD spouses feel (because they generally talk about it), it seems that ADHD spouses feel *even worse,* even if they don't adequately communicate it to their partners.

Evidence of this comes from some preliminary research done in 2002 by Dr. Arthur Robin and Eleanor Payson to help understand which behaviors have a negative impact on couples affected by ADHD. They asked 80 couples to rate a series of psychological statements related to feeling unloved, unimportant, or ignored. I expected to see results in this research that suggested that non-ADHD people felt unloved, having been in that position myself. I was surprised to find that the ratings for feeling unloved were higher in ADHD spouses than their non-ADHD partners![9]

How to explain, then, why they don't share these feelings with their partners more openly? I asked one of my clients this very question. He is what I might classify as a "man's man with a heart"--he holds a typically male job, hunts deer, and sometimes hangs out with the guys and "swaps lies." He also likes to talk about deep things with his spouse some of the time. To my surprise, he did not say something like "Men don't like to talk about their feelings." Instead, he told me the following:

> I believe that people with ADHD feel much more ignored and unloved than they let on completely. It's like an unintentional secret that we walk around with—your lot in life. You don't talk a lot about how unloved and unimportant you feel. Mostly you find a way to keep yourself pumped up because nobody else is going to do it. You buy into the idea that you'll amount to nothing because you "just don't get it" but you hide how unwanted you feel.

9. Arthur L. Robin and Eleanor Payson, "The Impact of ADHD on Marriage," *The ADHD Report*, 10 (3) 2002: 9-14.

My husband concurs. Although he didn't have these feelings growing up because he compensated so well for his ADHD, once our marriage started to deteriorate and I started to correct and nag him, one of his major feelings was that of being unappreciated and unloved. Of course, he never once told me about the "unloved" part. Think about the implications of this for a moment. Non-ADHD partners spend a good deal of time trying to instruct their ADHD spouses to do things differently and, often, to *be* different. At first this is well intentioned, but even this "help" reinforces the idea that "I don't want you as you are." One common non-ADHD partner theme is "If my partner would just *change*...." Yet a change in habits is most likely to happen when a person feels *loved and safe* within a relationship, just the opposite of the message that much of the daily communication between you sends.

Top Marital Issues That Both Partners Agree Lead to Feeling Unloved[10]

- Failing to remember what the other has said
- Talking without thinking
- Zoning out of conversations
- Having trouble dealing with frustration
- Having trouble getting started on a task
- Underestimating time needed to complete a task
- Leaving a mess
- Failing to finish household projects

In addition, ADHD partners rated "tolerating too much and blowing up inconsistently" and "trying to do too much in a short time" as top issues. Non-ADHD partners included "doesn't respond when spoken to" and "doesn't plan ahead."

10. Arthur L. Robin and Eleanor Payson, "The Impact of ADHD on Marriage," *The ADHD Report*, 10 (3) 2002: 9-14.

In spite of feeling unappreciated, or perhaps in part because of it, many with ADHD work hard to try to be accepted by their spouse. One man described the mental gymnastics he performs every day in order to not disappoint his partner:

> I think about what I'm going to do all the time—at work, at home, in my car. I admire my wife's standards, and try to meet them but often fall short. I often feel as if I'm just waiting for the other shoe to drop. Having come from an entire lifetime of "do it again" I've learned that it's a long road back. Sometimes the long road back seems almost endless and I just hook a right turn and go down another road then.

If you have ADHD but have never treated it, you tend to think that "the long road back" is just how life is…until you start successful treatment! One woman who was contemplating stopping her ADHD medication while she went through pregnancy explains here how her life changed after treatment. Now that she has pulled her life together in a way that makes her happier and is holding down a more complex job, she doesn't want to return to what she had before, which she likens to having the flu every day:

> [Having ADHD is like] when you have the flu but you need to go to work, so you go and you do your job, but every minute is a struggle. You can't think straight, you keep forgetting what you were doing, you make mistakes but every 5 minutes you have to give yourself a pep talk to keep going. That is what it feels like for me at work with no meds. The thought of having to do that for 1+ years between trying to have a baby and actually doing so is unbearable.

With the perspective of treatment, this woman now sees that her new life is quite different from her "flu" days. She is loath to go back to what she now sees as unnecessary suffering and effort. Since she can't take her stimulant medication during pregnancy without risk to the fetus, she has some difficult decisions to make.

Often, those who have found ways to treat their ADHD see their lives in a more positive light, and sometimes even see their ADHD as a plus. Here are the words of my now college-age daughter, who has been treating her ADHD with a variety of approaches since she was in fifth grade:

> Obviously there are challenges that we must overcome with ADHD. I started out being very disorganized, but I experimented through trial and error to see what methods of organization work best for me…I spend more time on my work than most of my friends, and really have to stay right on top of things…I've learned not only how to live with my ADHD, but I've come to appreciate just how important it is to who I am as a person. It's a big factor in why I'm creative, and how I see things differently from other people. I attribute all of these things to my ADHD and those are really important, positive parts of who I am. I wouldn't want to not have ADHD.

With behavioral and pharmacological treatment, my daughter got her organizational issues under control well enough to live her life as she chooses and be competitive at one of the best high schools (and now colleges) in the country.

If you are in the middle of a marital struggle, you may feel as if ADHD is always a bad thing. I would argue that ADHD was a big part of why we found our spouses attractive in the first place. A non-hierarchical ADHD brain can see things in new ways, which can in turn inspire creativity and entrepreneurship. The energy, spontaneity and joy with which many who have ADHD live their lives can be contagious. As one non-ADHD spouse put it, "While I think about the problems we have, I also try to remind myself that this is the same man who can break out into song and dance in the aisle at Walmart." The ADHD ability to move beyond adversity can also be a real gift. Quick recovery from setbacks might have been very appealing earlier in your relationship, even if it may currently (mis)communicate to you that your spouse doesn't care about your marital issues.

In a later section of the book I will urge you both to strengthen the boundaries that separate you. In doing so, it is critical that each of you take seriously the ADHD spouse's ideas and ways of doing things. This respect for all that is good, as well as difficult, elevates the ADHD spouse back to "partner" status and is an important part of creating an atmosphere in which your spouse is most likely to succeed.

The environment in which a person with ADHD lives is critical to success, ability to stay "unstuck," and ability to keep ADHD symptoms under control. Compare the experiences of these two people. The first lives with a wife who "was born without patience." The second lives with a man who laughs along with her at a new, somewhat wacky coping strategy:

> I'm a little disoriented most days. I need a list of things to do or nothing gets done. My wife just bit my head off for putting something in the wrong place and all I heard was an attack…I have a real problem on my hands. I've got ADHD pretty bad and she was born without patience. When we were first together we were inseparable and had a great time. But now that more and more responsibilities have been pouring in, I've started to drop the ball and I don't think that she is understanding what I am going through, despite her suggestions of getting on medication. So…I've been taking Adderall for a month now, to no avail. I'm beginning to feel a little down because she is aggressive and takes the reins from me and does not hesitate to tell me how irresponsible I am. I know this is all frustration

> speaking, but it still gets to me. I have tried to express to her that the only way for me to be able to take care of things is to give me a little more time (actively, i.e. when setting up our new internet through satellite, I asked the teller all sorts of questions and my wife huffed and rolled her eyes at me saying I'm and idiot for taking too long). The only reason I need more time doing things is because I feel I need to be more thorough or I haven't done anything at all. I do a lot of cleaning around the house and can do a lot of dishes at a time, but she is obviously not impressed by my speed, or lack thereof. I have now been labeled as: Lazy. I have a hard time understanding that statement since I break a sweat when I sweep the floor or need to drink extra water when I do laundry. I'm active. I did, to me, a lot of work. I'm not an idiot, I know she does the exact same thing but much faster. And maybe I'm OCD or something, cause to do the dishes is like surgery, I'm in there with precision tools and magnifying glasses.
>
> We've tried lists, but we both lose them. Calendars don't stay on walls. Egg timers have saved my butt a few times. My PDA is too involving to conquer. I get easily offended. Medication is apparently not working appropriately. I can't remember what I ate yesterday. My wife hates that I am so scattered. I hate that my wife is so scheduled. I never get to make any decisions in the house because she feels I am incapable…I want to know how to help myself…I have no attention span, poor time management and use the phrase, "I don't remember" a lot. My wife has zero patience, tolerance or time for any of this.

This man understands that things need to improve, and he also has a fairly good understanding of at least some of the ADHD symptoms that are getting in his way. But he is stuck. His medication isn't working, and he isn't going forward to find one that does. He does things around the house, like order Internet service, sweep the floor, and do dishes, but his wife's expectations that he'll do things as quickly as she does (and perhaps in the same way) sabotage his success. This means that even when he does contribute he isn't getting any positive feedback. In order to get out of the cycle they are in, they need marital counseling from an ADHD expert—a person who will help the husband optimize his ADHD treatment and help the wife understand the role that her behavior plays in their problems.

Here's a different experience:

> I am 42 with ADD. Before I started to take meds I had no concept of time. [My husband] would say you are too slow. When doing housework. Or any time. This hurt me very badly. When I started to take meds I was able to calculate better the concept of time. Before I had no clue of how much time would pass. When I started to take the meds I started to make cleaning fun by playing games with myself like setting the timer on my oven while I clean the kitchen. I give my self 15 minutes at a time. My husband would say what are you doing? I would tell him "I want to see how much I can get done in 15 minutes and try to beat the clock." He loved the idea.

What used to be an area of conflict for this woman—getting things done in a reasonable amount of time—has been overcome with the help of medications, a new coping strategy, and emotional support from her husband. She created a fun, original, and motivating way to address her need to do the chores. This is a good example where medication allows a creative, and very personal, approach to solving the problem. This woman didn't suddenly become the same as someone without ADHD, but she was able to create a system that worked for her, and she is clearly reveling in her newfound control over something that used to cause her great difficulty. She can now laugh and use words like "clueless" without concern, in part because her husband recognizes her accomplishment.

What I Love About My ADHD Spouse

Remembering the positives in your relationship is an important step in moving forward. Here is a glimpse of what some non-ADHD spouses love about their partners:

> My husband can turn anything into a game. So much of ADHD literature focuses on the negative aspects, we can forget just how creative they can be. No matter what sort of fit my kids are throwing, my husband can turn it into a game and get them on board.
>
> He's a great playmate for the kids. Being such a kid himself, not only is he able to play on their level, but he helps me to remember that they're only little once, for a brief window, and that I don't want to be remembered for doing chores while they're playing. His play helps me to reconnect with the child inside.

> My husband is very affectionate, little touches such as pats on the back or hugs are always available and if I should ask for such things he drops everything to provide.

> On weekends, he has a coffee ready for me when I wake up in the morning. He tolerates my "morning grumpies" and knows not to take any of my grousing personally until an hour after I get up. He shares my passion for random trivia. He has no problem with my odder personality quirks and even encourages some of them. He encourages me in my passions. His need to keep life interesting can really keep life interesting in a positive way.

What I Love... *continued*

My husband has a remarkable capacity to love and forgive, which is a gift for us all. I've learned to really appreciate his ability to take things in stride and respond flexibly to just about any situation. He is open to trying just about anything new that I might want to try, and his love of finding the next adventure keeps our lives interesting.

One strength I see in ADD is "bounce-back-ability." My partner can move from pain to joy as fast as a child with a cut knee and a bowl of ice cream. I'm amazed at how quickly he can put things behind him!

I love my husband's quirky sense of humor. I grew up in a household where humor was important, and not just everyday joking. I tend to take life a little *too* seriously sometimes, and I need his sense of the ridiculous to keep me on an even keel. But mostly I love that he is not boring.... My husband is still interesting to me after 35 years of marriage. Believe me, I do appreciate the irony of this—I'm sure he wouldn't be so interesting without his ADD!!!... When my husband and I were separated a few years ago, I never even considered dating other men—none of the men I knew were even remotely as interesting as my husband.

It's important to try to understand the experience of the ADHD spouse because it is completely unlike that of the non-ADHD spouse. A person with ADHD sees and experiences the world differently, solves problems differently, and gets treated by others quite differently. The ADHD spouse faces challenges every day that deserve the empathy—and patience—of the non-ADHD partner.

I am not recommending pity for the ADHD spouse or suggesting that non-ADHD people subjugate their lives to their spouse's ADHD simply because a life with ADHD can be challenging. People with ADHD have specific, and very real, differences. Their days are significantly harder than the non-ADHD partner realizes or the ADHD spouse admits. Life can be a series of unrelenting challenges for a partner with ADHD, particularly when he is not well positioned to take advantage of his strengths, such as in a household setting. A non-ADHD spouse must understand that it is not spitefulness, laziness, meanness, or lack of desire that keeps her husband from doing what she has requested. When he says, "I wanted to do that—I just forgot," it would be healthier for her to take "I wanted to do that" as seriously as she takes "I just forgot." And *he* needs to take that part seriously, too. ADHD isn't an excuse for continued incompetence. It's a diagnosis that indicates that specific types of treatments and habit changes will help a person pull his life together. Remember, the goal isn't to be non-ADHD, but to be able to be happy in your life and relationship of choice.

Talk with your ADHD spouse. Ask him or her what ADHD feels like. You may well be surprised to learn about hidden shame or anxieties, feeling overwhelmed, or the embarrassment of being constantly criticized. Your conversations about these things might help you to proceed in a way that communicates your love and your needs in a way that's more satisfying to you both.

Exercise: Write a Letter About Your ADHD

For the ADHD Spouse:

Grab your computer or a pad of paper, and start to brainstorm about your ADHD and experiences. It doesn't have to be highly organized. In fact, I like to think of this exercise as an "ADHD tone poem" – like music, or the strokes of a paintbrush – capturing in words the experience and images of your ADHD. Write a letter to your partner about what it feels like for you to live with ADHD and when you are ready, share it with your spouse. Keep this exercise about you and what your experience is, not about your spouse or your marriage. Later, if you find that this starts some meaningful conversations, you can focus on your relationship.

For the Non-ADHD Spouse:

This may be the beginning of some very important discussions. Don't offer "solutions" to the issues that your spouse might write about. Make the assumption that your spouse is not trying to create excuses, but rather to share with you his experience. He is not writing to get advice he's writing to help you learn about, and appreciate, him. Remain open, ask lots of probing questions and stay focused on your spouse, not on you or the state of your marriage. When you are done, make sure to say "thank you." Opening up can be hard to do.

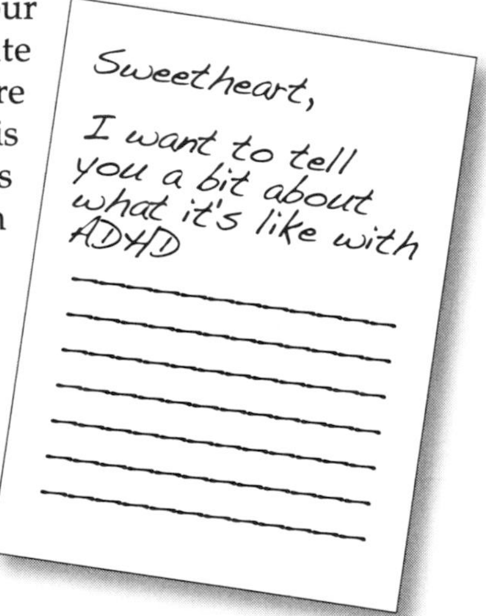

What It's Like to Be a Non-ADHD Spouse in Marital Crisis

What does the ADHD spouse need to understand about the experiences of the non-ADHD spouse? Perhaps the most important thing is that ADHD affects the non-ADHD spouse much more than can be imagined. ADHD symptoms are real to both spouses, albeit in a different way. Even if you didn't realize you had ADHD until recently, you were still dealing with the symptoms previous to diagnosis. Not so, the non-ADHD spouse. The impact of ADHD symptoms is *new* to the non-ADHD spouse, which means that he or she associates these difficult new experiences with *you as a person,* since they started when you entered his or her life.

As with the ADHD spouse, the non-ADHD experience runs along a spectrum from mildly problematic to unmanageable. At the milder end of the spectrum is a spouse who finds herself surprised and unhappy that her husband is not paying as much attention to her as he did when they were courting. She is trying to work through getting the two of them more emotionally aligned, and may be feeling frustrated. At the unmanageable end of the spectrum is the partner who feels completely overburdened by the responsibilities she has assumed because she thinks her spouse can't do them. She dislikes herself when she is with her husband, and she dislikes her husband. She may be seething in anger, incapable of holding a civil conversation, and anxious or resentful any time she gets near the bedroom. This is the stage I was in some years ago. You *can* come back from this stage to a happy and healthy marriage.

In general, the experience of a non-ADHD spouse is a predictable *progression* from happy to confused to angry to hopeless. In overview, the non-ADHD spouse often experiences the following feelings:

- **Lonely**. The ADHD spouse is too distracted to pay attention.
- **Unwanted or unloved**. The lack of attention is interpreted as lack of interest rather than distraction. One of the most common dreams is to be "cherished," and to receive the attention from one's spouse that this implies.

- **Angry and emotionally blocked**. Anger and resentment permeate many interactions with the ADHD spouse. Sometimes this anger is expressed as disconnection. In an effort to control angry interactions, some non-ADHD spouses try to block their feelings by bottling them up inside.
- **Incredibly stressed out.** Non-ADHD spouses often carry the vast proportion of the family responsibilities and can never let their guard down. Life could fall apart at any time because of the ADHD spouse's inconsistency.
- **Ignored and offended.** To a non-ADHD spouse, it doesn't *make sense* that the ADHD spouse doesn't act on the non-ADHD partner's experience and advice more often when it's "clear" what needs to be done.
- **Scared**. The non-ADHD spouse tends to fear for the couple's children, worrying that a distracted spouse will somehow hurt the kids; and for oneself, that life will continue along its current and difficult path. Some non-ADHD spouses fantasize about leaving because the current path feels unsustainable.
- **Exhausted and depleted**. The non-ADHD spouse carries too many responsibilities, and no amount of effort seems to fix the relationship. There appears to be a gender difference to this feeling: Male non-ADHD spouses are less likely to try to compensate for an ADHD wife's lack of organization, and so are less likely to be exhausted. They also seem to move to divorce earlier.
- **Frustrated.** A non-ADHD spouse might feel as if the same issues keep coming back over and over again (a sort of boomerang effect). This is a new experience. In the past, problems generally got "taken care of," and the partner moved on to the next issue.
- **Hopeless and sad.** Many dreams have been put aside, and a profound grief pervades the daily difficulties of life.

The progressive nature of the non-ADHD spouse's experience explains why many ADHD spouses feel that the non-ADHD partner has changed for the worse. However, if you look at the non-ADHD experience, you can understand why the spouse is different now:

> When my husband started to "grow back into" his ADD in his late 30s, it was initially very bewildering. He had always been thoughtful before, and now he seemed so thoughtless and self-centered. He became more and more inconsistent. I was at a loss to understand what was happening and therefore distressed and worried. As his behaviors became more pronounced, his increasing "carelessness" and "thoughtlessness" started to become physically and financially dangerous to himself and to our children. I stopped worrying about why he was behaving differently because I was too busy being very scared for their safety and our future. I would tell him how scared I was, and his reaction was always that he would never do anything to hurt us—he couldn't see at all that he could hurt us through negligence.
>
> From fear I progressed to anger (I'd been brought up to get mad instead of cry). We'd talked so often about the problem behaviors and how upset they made me and the effect he was having on the kids, and yet he was still doing them! It seemed to me that he wasn't listening, he wasn't caring, he wasn't thinking, and that seemed really irresponsible and it made me very mad. And it seemed like he listened better and thought more when I yelled! So I yelled more and more, which fed my anger further.
>
> Around this time my husband was finally diagnosed with ADD. For various reasons, progress was extremely slow, which was depressing for me. I knew it wasn't realistic but I wanted a silver bullet. I spent a lot of time in despair that we would ever have a non-dysfunctional family life. I was also very lonely. Nobody understood what I was coping with—his family was in

> denial about the whole thing, and my family just didn't "get it." I didn't have any friends that weren't also friends with my husband, and he's so charming in public (and had fewer opportunities to show his more troubling behaviors) that nobody understood what I was coping with.
>
> By the time we finally did work out solutions, I felt my life had been shredded beyond recognition, although I do understand that life isn't obligated to fulfill our expectations! What has made me sad is that I always felt I had some special abilities to bring to the service of many people while I earned a living, and while I have managed to do some good things for a few people over the course of my life, I don't feel like I accomplished anywhere near as much as I could have. Today, through a lot of work and better meds, my marriage is happy again; I am a stronger and hopefully wiser person; but I am scarred forever.

Non-ADHD spouses will probably note how familiar this progression of emotions seems. The progression happens in response to specific ADHD symptoms—his distraction inspired her worry, then fear. Continuation of distraction and disconnection led to her anger and yelling to get his attention. This is a good example of the action–reaction cycle when ADHD goes undiagnosed and untreated. The good news is that this couple is now living happily together again. *Her* final step, though, would be to reconnect with her dreams of being of service to others so she could feel greater personal fulfillment and treasure her life in its full breadth and depth.

I mentioned feeling lonely as a key component of the non-ADHD experience. Loneliness comes from many things: the distraction of the ADHD, which makes the non-ADHD partner feel ignored and unloved; a sense that the non-ADHD spouse carries such a disproportionate amount of the responsibility without input from the ADHD partner; a sense of never being "heard" since so many patterns are repeated; and the fact that few people outside the marriage "see" what is going on. Sex often becomes strained, adding to disconnection:

> I can completely identify with the anger and resentment issues! I've seen some people post that their ADD spouse has no sex drive, but what if it's the other way around?? I have almost no interest in sex these days. I feel like I am caring for a child. And feeling motherly (and resentful) does not do a whole lot for feeling amorous. We have been married now for 5 1/2 years and I cannot remember feeling more lonely.

Loneliness can also result from being married to a person who often seems to be "self-contained." One characteristic of having ADHD can be that you are "off in your own world" much of the time. This behavior creates distance between the two spouses, leaving the non-ADHD partner feeling alone.

> At times I become overwhelmed by the sadness and mourning for the relationship I *could* have with my spouse if he did not have ADHD. I love him very much but I think about how much easier our lives, my life, would be if he did not have ADHD. It is lonely being the only person in a relationship who remembers and takes care of the mundane, who builds on goals for the future, and who self-monitors.

A spouse without ADHD may be competent enough to manage the logistics of the household, but the stress of doing so alone creates angry, hurt feelings and disconnection. Here is another moving description:

> We've been together 5 years, married 4. Four kids — mine (age 14), his (ADHD – 9) and ours (3). My husband is my 42 year old child. When I met him I had hobbies and things I loved to do. For the most part, those things are gone. Normally I'm the main breadwinner; right now I'm the only breadwinner. I do 95% of the

> housework, child care, and the errands of life. I gave up my hobbies because there is just no time left for me. I tried to keep one hobby for awhile, which was taking dance lessons one night a week. I had to give that up when my husband jeopardized our relationship with our babysitter because he could not manage to arrive to pick up the little ones on time. My husband keeps up his hobbies and mostly plays on the computer.
>
> There are so many things I could say to express how I feel about being in this relationship. Truly I think I could write a book. Sadness, rage, utter frustration, absolute exhaustion. They all seem to manifest themselves in a profound grief. I have battled suicidal feelings, but I simply could never do that to my children nor my parents, and I cannot imagine my husband trying to parent our little ones alone. The thought frightens me into keeping myself going no matter what.
>
> That's not to say that there is nothing good. My husband is a gentle soul, very kind and tender. If he were not like that, we would not still be together. Sometimes we still have fun together. Sometimes I have glimpses of the joy and passion of our first year together. My life with my ADD husband is sort of like living in a rainy climate. It's mostly gray and dreary, but once in awhile the sun comes out and the world is beautiful and sparkly for awhile.

The inconsistency of living with ADHD is an important theme. Just as inconsistency can cripple the ADHD spouse's faith in his competence, so too does it affect the non-ADHD spouse. If you don't know whether you can rely on your partner to pick up the baby from the sitter's, you experience a good deal of stress until the question is resolved each day. At any time, you might be the one who gets to "clean up" from something left unfinished or forgotten. Thus the non-ADHD spouse can never relax. She learns to mistrust her spouse, because while his intentions are usually good, his untreated (or under-treated) ADHD gets in the way of his turning intention into action.

Always needing to be on alert, combined with being responsible for the majority of all of the chores and scutwork, results in exhaustion. If you are an ADHD spouse and your non-ADHD spouse snaps at you about everything, there are probably two reasons: your partner is exhausted and has discovered that snapping and yelling is one of the most effective ways to get your attention.

One of the reasons that non-ADHD partners suffer is that they have very little control over what is happening to them. Yes, they might be able to moderate their responses (and should), but the general outline of their lives is dictated not by themselves, but by their spouses' ADHD and whether it is being effectively managed. This is a bittersweet concept, particularly if the ADHD partner is still in denial that the ADHD matters:

> My husband is a super guy: wonderful, sweet, romantic, generous, loving, hard-working, kind, compassionate. But all of these qualities disappear when we run up against issues where his ADD holds court in strength. A general, common scenario: Situation A would present itself (anything from a little issue to a huge one), which would require action B on his part and action C on mine. Assuming that I could get his attention for a few moments, we would come to conclusions about what needed to be done, I would do action C…and he would go off thinking about and doing something else. I would later point B out to him, and he would say he would do it. We'd come back to the issue long after this point, and he would tell me he'd still get around to it, tell me he "never said" he would do it, get angry at me, shut down, or threaten to leave (even over little issues). The result would be that either I would have to give up and leave the issue unresolved, or do B myself (if I could), and be very unhappy that I was doing "my" work and "his" in the marriage.
>
> Repeat this scenario, daily, and you can get an idea of how unhappy life had become for me. It was like

> living with a perennial toddler. A wonderful, sweet, generous, loving, hard-working, etc. toddler who had a very odd view of reality and what marriage was about, and (again, because of his disorder) did exactly what he felt like every moment of the day and looked out for number 1 at the expense of those around him.
>
> I cannot emphasize enough that these are *not* his personal qualities—they're actually the *opposite* of his true nature. But when he lets his ADD be in charge—which has become more and more often over time—it's as though he's trapped way in there somewhere, and on the outside I have to deal with an entirely different person. This "ADD guy" is *not* someone I want to be married to. He's the one who did so much damage to me and our marriage, and I am furious at what he did to my wonderful husband. But "ADD guy" is in charge now, and there's nothing I can do about it.

This woman is able to separate her husband from his symptoms. But her experience is that the symptoms are still in control. Notice the role that the chore wars play in her life. It is her inability to rely on her husband in their daily interactions that has started a spiral that undoubtedly includes both his ADHD characteristics and her "furious" negative responses to those symptoms. But other ADHD traits also affect her—his lack of impulse control (angry rages over small things); inability to organize and initiate tasks; and living in the moment. There is a sad and hopeless note to her "and there's nothing I can do about it." He must take better control of his symptoms, or this marriage will likely end.

Lack of control is critical to the experience of the non-ADHD spouse, and after a while it completely wears her down:

> When we first married I dreamed of the two of us being a team...tackling problems together, building a life together, growing together, supporting each other, being equals...and so on. I anticipated the day to day marital

> problems, but was ill prepared for the problems that came with my husband's ADHD. I realized early on in the marriage that something wasn't quite right, but I couldn't understand what was going on. My husband wasn't supportive, he was distant and unemotional, he leaned heavily on alcohol and a host of other problems. I began to feel confused, frustrated, and very disappointed. I kept thinking, "How could this be my life?" "Why did he bring this (his problems) into my life?" When you're in an ADHD marriage (especially with a spouse who hasn't been diagnosed) everything spins out of control. You try hard to wrap your arms around it all, to regain control, but it's futile. No matter how strong you started out, you feel weaker from the journey. In many ways, your initial dreams become just that...dreams. You don't have the energy to pursue them anymore.

The "spinning out of control" idea sounds just like how many with ADHD describe their brains and lives, doesn't it?

Here is another description of how much living with ADHD wears one down:

> Over the years, I have brought [my husband with ADHD] to one kind of marriage counseling after another. No change. He loves to sit with people and talk, but nothing changes after the meeting is over. I am extremely hurt by it all. And I still feel very alone. He will not change; he cannot change. In his never-ending-last-minute-emergency-drop/go-never-available-for-me life, I can hardly catch his attention. He is always too busy, and never can make time for me. I am just the big kill-joy wife who is always putting a damper on his fun because I am thinking of the practical things that need to be done while he is thinking of all the fun things he wants to do when he isn't at work. Yes, it gets old. No, I don't know

> what to do about it...I am tired of repeatedly having my hopes dashed.... To sum up, if it all depends on me, then I guess I am just not a big enough person to do it. I can do a lot, and maybe I can do more than many other people, but I cannot do everything.

This woman's description covers so much: the loss of hope, her attempts to "fix" her marriage that haven't paid off, her feelings of loneliness, hurt, and, yes, resentment. Her description is full of her spouse's ADHD symptoms and reflects the conflicts they have endured as a couple as he has been forever busy while she has unhappily fallen into the role of organizer and "killjoy." She has lost faith in herself and her ability to change her life because she feels held hostage by his symptoms.

To a person with ADHD, one of the defining characteristics of their non-ADHD partner is anger—and lots of it. I will be writing about anger in depth in the next chapter, so I won't delve deeply here, but chronic anger is one of the defining experiences for many non-ADHD spouses. And it's not just anger at their spouse, but also at themselves.

Here is how one woman describes her own self-loathing at what she feels she has become:

> Being married to an ADD husband makes you doubt yourself, and hate yourself because of the negative thoughts you have for your husband. I, for one, am about to lose my mind. While I know my husband has ADD, I feel like the problem is with ME...that I don't have enough patience, enough optimism, enough creativity. I feel like I am a stick in the mud while my husband is the fun happy-go-lucky guy that everybody loves. I watch people adore my husband and all the while I think to myself, "Yea, but you don't have to live with him." Being married to an ADD husband is like being married to a child that everyone loves but who you are sick and tired of...it puts you in a "mother" role. And let me tell you I HATE that.

Self-loathing in an important concept to understand for the non-ADHD spouse, because dealing with it constructively by taking back control of one's life is an important element in turning things around.

> I know that I have done things wrong in this marriage, too. I have allowed him to manipulate me with his anger. I have taken over the role of mother to him. I do not like who I am when I am with him…a person full of repressed anger and very little joy for life. In my effort to not yell and scream at his ADD behaviors I have repressed not only my anger, but my other emotions as well. As I respond to others in the family, I find that there is not much enthusiasm on my part to do things or be as involved as I'd like to be.

This woman would benefit from talking with her doctor about the possibility that she may be suffering from situational depression that would benefit from treatment ("I find that there is not much enthusiasm on my part to do things"). Rather than suppressing her feelings, she needs a constructive way to express them, perhaps with the help of a counselor.

As frustration and anger build, non-ADHD spouses can start making less empathetic decisions, sometimes abdicating responsibility for helping a spouse in practical and easy ways while trying to push him in harder areas so he can "prove" his love. This serves the dual purpose of punishing him further and proving herself correct.

> For my 34th birthday a couple of weeks ago, I asked my husband for a nice meal out & a movie. It didn't happen. He took a nap & by the time he woke up, it was past our reservation. I am tired of all the disappointments. Even when I ask for things I'd like for special occasions—it rarely happens.

It would not have been hard for this woman to wake her husband from his nap in time to go to dinner. But she is tired of being responsible all the time. By not waking him she can blame him further for her disappointments. One cannot argue that it was her *responsibility* to wake him up, but were she feeling charitable she could easily have done so. Instead she chose the path that would produce the greatest amount of hard feelings for them both. It is unfortunate, but some of the time a non-ADHD spouse is subtly and unknowingly sabotaging the relationship at the same time as complaining that the spouse cannot change. This isn't intentional, but it is a sign of frustration that is becoming unmanageable. This behavior is the mirror of the ADHD spouse who sabotages the relationship by refusing to undertake serious treatment for ADHD.

In addition to hopeless and angry, another good word to describe a typical non-ADHD spouse is *exhausted*.

> Our daughter is now almost five. I have never been able to spend the time with her that I think she deserves. She goes to daycare 5 days a week which I pay for out of my very meager paycheck—and that supports the three of us while my husband completes his PhD. He has had repeated setbacks in finalizing but now there is hope in sight. We are now at the point of cleaning out any retirement savings we ever had in order to live. I do the cooking, cleaning, housework, enrichment activity planning for our daughter, shuttling her around, bathing, dressing, and drop off to school. And hold down my fulltime job in a severely dysfunctional work environment that I feel I must keep (frankly, I feel trapped) due to the economic conditions we are all living in right now. At night, after I make dinner (if we want to eat healthfully I HAVE to cook), I get our daughter set up for bed and put her down.
>
> Almost every single night I have to remind my husband that bedtime is NOT the time to start laughing, joking, tickling or roughhousing. I not only seem to have the bulk of the parenting and household duties but I get sabotaged along the way.

> I want to be tolerant and accepting, I really do, but after 5+ years of living like this I am at my emotional wits end. My husband is a good man but I don't feel at all warm or loving to him anymore. Just parental. Or servant to master. If I don't do the household tasks he gets on a rant about the house being dirty, or the dishes laying around. I feel very much damned if I do or damned if I don't.
>
> I am not enjoying life anymore. My happiest times are when he has an evening class and I can play with my daughter and put her to bed after without any additional drama. I often feel as though I'm a single parent of 2 kids.

As you can see, much that should be present in a good, healthy relationship is missing. One could suggest that this woman could relax and play with her husband and daughter, but after the intensity of her day and with the burden of feeling disconnected, it just doesn't sound appealing.

Many non-ADHD spouses can't believe how much their relationship has changed. It is intensely frustrating to watch the changes happen, and to feel helpless about doing anything to fix the worsening problems. Then treatment starts and hope is renewed. Finally, there is a "name" for what has been happening! But treating ADHD takes time, as it includes both physiological and habit changes. While it's a relief to start treatment, all too often one or both spouses believe that medication *alone* will act as a sort of magic pill. If treatment is limited to medication, results are usually suboptimal and disappointing. Medication is only one element of treatment. Here's a woman who describes the frustration of dealing with incomplete treatment:

> Eight years ago I married THE ONE for me. Awesome guy in every respect and focused on our relationship (even when it was only a friendship) to a very flattering degree. As many of you have experienced, this focus changed a couple years into our marriage and hurt my

feelings quite a bit. Other than that, which we dealt with through both healthy communication and some angry fights (which sometimes seem the only way to make him genuinely aware of a situation), things went pretty smoothly until about 3 years ago. My husband describes the phases of our marriage as "Man this is a blast" to "A few things we could work on to be a more successful couple" to "things that NEED to be worked on now" to finally hitting "WHY AREN'T THESE THINGS WE'VE DISCUSSED OVER AND OVER EVER GETTING DONE?!!??!?"

My anger and disappointment built steadily, and it vented at him loudly when he failed ONCE AGAIN to do what he had agreed to (possibly because he cheerfully agrees to everything asked by anyone).... His only answer after the same discussions and arguments over and over was perhaps something was wrong with him. Now I am married to a HIGHLY functioning ADD person...so I didn't put much stock in maybe he had "something wrong." He just seemed to be a person who enjoyed fun things more than unfun things. Welcome to the human race—suck it up. I finally told him that I was sick of hearing the same old "maybe" thing and if he really thought something could be wrong, go to the doctor, figure it out, but for heaven's sake DO SOMETHING about it...he was diagnosed with ADD 2 years ago. He was relieved to find out there was a reason for so many things that seemed inexplicable—he is practically a genius yet flunked out of college because he couldn't/wouldn't bother going to class. No ability or desire to organize himself at all. Naturally he married a woman who LOVES organization...I swear in the beginning no non-ADD spouse could have been more supportive than I was, but we are 2 years into this process and I feel like almost no change has taken place. I think he wanted the pills to be a magic bullet and that

> he wasn't going to have to put any work into it himself. My patience is fast fading. I do not expect this to ever not be part of our lives, and we honestly have ourselves some great laughs about it at times, but so often it feels like he isn't trying at all. He genuinely thinks that THINKING about making a change counts as trying. Ok fine—in the beginning count thinking and organizing yourself as trying, but 2 years later he is still THINKING about it??? I mean I bring perfectionism to the table which I know is no picnic for him, and he seldom complains; but I feel the difference is that I am actively working on it.

It is no surprise that with all of this stress, some non-ADHD spouses fantasize about leaving:

> I dream of stability, mature decision making, taking responsibility for one's own actions ...a day where there are no phone calls to our home for overdue payments of some kind...where calmness resides and there is some sort of structure...where I am not blamed for things, because there is someone else in the household...who...will take responsibility for his own behaviors instead of turning it around to me!... He's on his 11th job search in our 5 year marriage. Yet, he claims if I wasn't so upset at his job losses...things would run more smoothly.... Please forgive me, for if I sound angry...I am, I don't know what to do and wish I were well enough to leave, I wish I didn't feel so sorry for him, or feel I am obligated, because of marriage vows...because I really think I would do it...leave!

Many non-ADHD spouses find themselves bereft of any ideas on how to improve their lives. In essence, under the symptom–response–response patterns of the ADHD effect, they find themselves stuck, with leaving the only way forward:

> [My husband is] convinced that it was me. He's even told his friends and family that it was me, and I can't even begin to tell you how much this hurt.... He won't see an ADD specialist, I think partially because he doesn't want to be told that his mental disorder caused the disintegration of our marriage. I don't think he could take that, so he stays with a non-ADD therapist who tells him what he wants to hear.
>
> I've very recently given up on him. Not just on the marriage—on my husband as a person. He's not a horrible man, but his condition—and his approach to dealing with it (or, more accurately, not dealing with it)-—will be the death of me, and I have to get away from him. For months, I thought it was my job to "save" him and "save" my marriage, but I was getting so hurt from all of the misplaced blame.... He has a condition, he knows he has a condition, and he's learned enough to know that it's what wreaked so much havoc in our lives and hurt me (and him) so deeply. For him to scapegoat me and to refuse to take responsibility for himself is more than I'm willing to endure.

Effective treatment, used in the broadest sense of the word, can change the life of an ADHD spouse. It also radically changes the life of the non-ADHD partner. For me, the difference that my husband's medication and behavioral changes make is huge. We are completely stable and happy now, because we have found strategies to accommodate ADHD, relearned how to trust each other to be affectionate and loving, and made sure we carve time out of our busy lives to focus on each other. But I was reminded of the role that medication plays in that balance when, two years into treatment, my husband decided to stop taking his medication for a week to see if he still needed it. Luckily, he warned me he was going to do this. At one point during the week he started yelling at me out of the blue. I began to fight back, then recognized the old pattern. "Listen to yourself right now," I said. "You haven't attacked me like this since you started your medication." He was able to reflect on my comment, rather than be defensive about it, and started taking his medications again that evening.

It takes time to find the balance that my husband and I have found. Just as it is unrealistic to expect that people with ADHD can just "turn off" their ADHD symptoms, it is also unrealistic to expect that non-ADHD spouses can just "turn off" their response to their own experiences with ADHD.

> I have been reading nonstop all week about adult ADD and tips/guidelines on how to work around this in a marriage. I find I am having a huge problem switching my thinking to that of "this is a handicap and needs to be treated as such." I do truly believe the diagnosis, but have so much anger and resentment that has built up over the past 6 years and I fear I will never be able to let it go. I did not ask to be married to someone with this disorder, I did not expect my life to take this turn. I know my husband loves me, but I feel resentment that I have to schedule time for him to remember to show me… I truly love my husband and I DO want to stay married to him. I am willing to do what it takes to make that happen, but I AM STILL SO ANGRY!

You can know intellectually about your anger and know how different you are and still have trouble knowing what to do next. I'm going to ask you to step outside of yourselves—or perhaps dig deeper into yourselves, if you prefer to think of it this way—and ask that you BOTH step out of your current cycle. Will it be easy? I think you can see that it will not be easy for either of you. But it is critical that you break the circular, reinforcing negatives of your relationship.

Step 2: Addressing Obstacle Emotions

"If we feel chronically angry or bitter in an important relationship, this is a signal that too much of the self has been compromised and we are uncertain about what new position to take or what options we have available to us. To recognize our lack of clarity is not a weakness but an opportunity, a challenge, and a strength."
— Harriet Lerner, *The Dance of Anger*

The common patterns in ADHD relationships lead partners to experience specific and predictable emotions. For example, it is likely that in response to an ADHD spouse's inconsistency the non-ADHD spouse will experience disappointment or lose faith. An ADHD partner is likely to feel resentment if bossed around all the time by a frustrated non-ADHD "parent" partner.

Four particular emotions must be acknowledged early in the rebuilding process. I call them *obstacle emotions,* for if left unattended they block couples from being able to move in a positive direction. They are

- fear of failure,
- chronic anger,
- denial, and
- hopelessness.

Fear of Failure Can Paralyze

Several of the people with ADHD who have been quoted thus far have spoken eloquently of their fear of failure. Treating ADHD fully is one way to start to overcome this fear. As the proportion of successes to failures begins to improve, the fear of failure can begin to recede.

At the risk of infuriating non-ADHD partners, I will also say that the tone of the relationship is a critical factor in overcoming an ADHD partner's often deeply felt fear of failure. Often, in frustration, a non-ADHD partner points out every failure the ADHD spouse encounters and uses it as further proof of incompetence. A better way is to acknowledge failures as part of the experimentation needed to move forward. The former produces paralysis; the latter encourages experimentation.

This suggestion can be tough for the non-ADHD spouse to take. "I've tried to just let things go and remain neutral, but then nothing gets better! Why should I have to lower my standards?" The fear that no interference will mean no change is valid. But I'm suggesting something different here: not giving in or lowering standards, but creating a different type of interference with ADHD symptoms. One that acknowledges ADHD, validates the very real issues that ADHD partners face, and incorporates ADHD-sensitive coping strategies so that both can negotiate a better relationship. You've read about many of these strategies so far in this book, and there are more to come.

I will circle back to the idea of changing the environment in your marriage without giving up on your own needs. It's a critical component of overcoming not only the obstacle emotion fear of failure, but also its partner emotions anger and denial.

The Inevitability of Anger in ADHD Relationships

One of the best resources on the topic of anger is Harriet Lerner's book *The Dance of Anger: A Woman's Guide to Changing the Patterns of Intimate Relationships.* I strongly urge you both to read it. But first, let me give you some perspective on how to put what Lerner says into the context of the ADHD relationship.

All anger, Lerner writes, is to be respected. Anger is simply a warning sign that things are not going as they should. It is not the anger itself that is the issue; it is how we respond to that anger that is important. Unfortunately, because anger often stems from issues related to untreated ADHD symptoms, it's difficult to respond appropriately to diminish anger until the symptoms are addressed, because the underlying irritant remains. The result is that in many ADHD-affected relationships, anger virtually paralyzes one or both spouses.

But why is anger so common in ADHD relationships? While not speaking specifically about ADHD, Lerner offers some insight:

> Anger is inevitable when our lives consist of giving in and going along; when we assume responsibility for other people's feelings and reactions; when we relinquish our primary responsibility to proceed with our own growth and ensure the quality of our own lives; when we behave as if having a relationship is more important than having a self.[11]

Stop! I want you to read that quote again and think about how accurately it reflects not only your own life, but that of your ADHD spouse. You are both "giving in and going along" (albeit in different ways), you are both maintaining your relationship in spite of your unhappiness, and you have both stopped nurturing yourselves in ways that promote healthy individual growth. In these conditions, your anger is *inevitable* and will continue to be so until you take control and change your way of being together.

It's tempting to say, "If I just try harder, we can overcome this." In fact, this is the path that most adults pursue. ADHD spouses often live their lives as a campaign of good intentions that go unfulfilled. But trying harder doesn't work very well until you address the underlying symptoms. Non-ADHD spouses "try harder" by adjusting and adjusting, taking on more and more, until they are completely exhausted and hopeless. Here's one example:

11. Lerner, Harriet, *The Dance of Anger: A Woman's Guide to Changing the Patterns of Intimate Relationships*, HarperCollins, 2005, p. 6.

I've been married to my husband 8 years this month. Although we have 2 children age 4 and 2, I often feel like I have a third child who is 35. He has not been diagnosed, but everything fits, everything. I haven't spoken to any of our friends or family about this because I don't want to make him seem like a bad guy (I love him). But I am so exhausted, in every aspect of my life. It seems like we go in cycles. Months and months go by then finally I reach my breaking point, and we have a huge fight. Then he plugs in, he cleans up and does the things he should be doing, and that last for a few weeks, then slowly he starts fading out, I start picking up his slack and it starts all over again… I ask and beg for him to do more, he tells me I'm making him feel guilty because he only works 3 days. Trying to carry on a conversation with him is tiring, he constantly interrupts or answers prematurely. If we go out and he's had too many drinks he becomes very aggravated and agitated and I am on the receiving end of that. In addition to our jobs, we own our own business, he procrastinates with calling people and doing things. I'm so tired trying to keep track of my own life as well as his.

I feel like I am in a constant state of frustration and exhaustion, which is directly affecting our intimate relationship. I just don't want to have sex, it feels like it's another chore, or another thing "he" needs, and what about my needs? Outside of hugs, he only touches me when he wants sex. Now it's to a point I don't even want him to touch me because I know what it's going to lead to. We are caught up in a vicious cycle. He agrees that he probably has ADD, but has yet to seek help or guidance about it. He has said he will, but hasn't yet.

I'm sorry if this post is a ramble, but I'm totally crying my eyes out as I'm typing this. I love my husband and can't picture my life without him, but at the same token, I can't see myself lasting much longer in the state I'm in.

This marriage shows all of the classic signs of an ADHD marriage: a parent–child dynamic; waves of frustration, anger, and exhaustion; denial that ADHD is a factor; sexual issues; and feelings of hopelessness in spite of underlying love.

If you've been trying hard for years now and things haven't changed, listen to your experience. *What you have been doing is not working.* You don't need to try *harder*, you need to try *differently*. I'm going to suggest that you make a radical shift in your thinking and behavior. One good way to begin is to think in terms of creating a completely new relationship. Put the old relationship in a box and put it aside. Then, create a new relationship in which you and your spouse work together on "today" and "tomorrow." Make today's progress more important than yesterday's failures. This method of starting over, when done together, can be an effective way to get out of the cycle of giving in and going along that propels you toward anger and away from love.

Before we get to the specific shift I'm recommending, I want to more fully explore the topic of anger.

Letting Go of Your Anger

You can effectively let go of your anger by putting aside your grudges and your rage. This enables you to take control and take responsibility for your own happiness. In so doing, you diminish the reasons your spouse might have to resist change in your relationship.

Here are the words of a woman who found that forgiving her spouse and letting go of her own anger turned out to be very productive:

> …your anger and resentment is something I really can relate to. I have been in some very, very dark places where those feelings have consumed me to the point of being ill. Not only did I feel the relationship was over, I felt my resentment was so deep and so unresolved, that no one could help me. The layers and layers of anger and resentment were so engulfing, and then I'd be so angry that the first issue was never resolved properly

> and now issue #3,456 has happened. One piece of advice I kept getting was to "let it go…" and I felt that the next person who said that to me was going to have my fist in their face because that "let it go" sounded more like "let him walk all over you" or "he gets a free pass" or "your strife really isn't that important" or "why are you making such a big deal about it" or "you don't get any validation."
>
> I believe strongly that each person must find what works for them—what works for one person may do nothing for another. But I do want to share that, to my total surprise and wonderment, I did find a way to let go that works for me, and it's done wonders for me. It includes knowing that if I choose to let go, I can choose to take back—and I can take back any time, that I am in control of this letting go thing, I make the rules for myself. And I get to just say no to letting go of certain things if I choose….

It may be counterintuitive, but letting go of your anger—essentially forgiving yourself and your spouse for your past—is a gift to yourself that frees you to move forward. As the person just quoted explained, "letting go" isn't ceding control, it's taking control. She has started to become independent of her husband again and is finding the pleasure of being in greater control of her own life.

Six Dangerous Myths About Anger

You might have trouble envisioning how you might be able to overcome your anger. If so, it could be that you are falling victim to some destructive myths about anger and ADHD.

Myth 1— I Can't Help It—My Spouse Drives Me to It

Sure you can! There is no doubt that your spouse's ADHD symptoms can create a huge burden. But anger is the result of taking too much responsibility for our spouse's feelings and reactions and not enough responsibility for our own life. You can address the root causes of anger in your relationship by giving back the responsibility for fixing ADHD to the partner who has it, while at the same time taking charge of your own happiness again. You can also train yourself to express your anger in positive and useful ways.

It can be scary to give back the responsibility for ADHD to a partner whom you suspect to be incapable of successfully navigating that responsibility. But perhaps you are beginning to see that the non-ADHD spouse can't "fix" a partner's ADHD. Although scary, the only real choice is to let your spouse responsible for his or her issues and to accept responsibility only for your own. You can (and should) be loving and supportive, and can give the "gift" of assistance when appropriate, as long as you are not taking responsibility. As soon as you feel you "must" take certain things on and don't really want to, resentment and anger will follow.

Myth 2—My Anger Will Force My Partner to Change

No, it won't. It hasn't yet. The things that you are angry about are the result of dealing with ADHD symptoms, which take time, effort, and support to manage. You can scare an ADHD person into changing temporarily, but you can't force it to last. You win the battle, but lose the war. Nature's response to anger is defensiveness and more anger. The poisonous environment that anger creates is just the opposite of the supportive and safe environment that an ADHD person needs in order to be successful. Not only will your anger not force a change, it will virtually assure that it doesn't occur.

Myth 3—My Partner Deserves It

Anger is a sign that things are out of balance, and this in turn can indicate that things must change. On the other hand, verbal abuse, screaming, belittling, shutting down, and shutting out are forms of punishment and bullying. No one "deserves" to be punished by a spouse.

Myth 4—Getting It All Out Will Make Me Feel Better

Releasing a short burst of anger *can* be an effective way to release bad feelings. But we're not talking about a short burst of anger. We're talking about pervasive, "can't get it out of my system" anger. And the reason that releasing the anger doesn't make you feel better over time is that the anger is caused by how you are both reacting to ADHD symptoms and interacting as a couple. If you don't fix the problem (and by "problem" I mean your joint ability to deal with symptoms and each other), releasing anger won't make either of you feel better; it will just repeatedly return and make you both feel worse.

Myth 5—If I Feel Hopeless, I Should Disconnect

You may be utterly exhausted, but disconnection isn't the solution. Although some claim it is the only way to bear the pain, the downside is that the pain is still there. And disconnection never makes a good marriage. Don't disconnect; seek help.

Myth 6—If I Deny My ADHD, the Problems Will Go Away

ADHD is built into the body and can't be made to "go away." The symptoms will persist until you deal with them effectively with treatment, preferably with a multipronged approach.

ADHD Symptoms and Anger

Some expressions of anger in ADHD spouses are the direct result of ADHD symptoms, and it makes sense to expose those here. When you come across these, tell yourself, "That's ADHD speaking," and don't escalate the experience.

Arguing About Little Things

Perhaps because their brains don't easily arrange things into a hierarchy, thus making everything seem "equal," a person with ADHD may pick completely trivial things to argue about, or even argue about *how* to argue. You know this argument isn't worth having, but you get caught up in it anyway. My husband used to drive me *nuts* when he would argue over whether I had used a word correctly while arguing with him! Usually, the underlying issue isn't the "little thing" you think you are fighting about. It's about who is in control or whether both partners feel respected:

> It's not that he doesn't understand the word I've used or my sentiment, it's that the word was WRONG and I should have known it would upset him. Even if he looks

> it up in the dictionary and sees I used it correctly, he maintains that I know how he would take it, therefore I was wrong to use it.... In addition, I (can) rephrase my sentiment any number of ways, but it always comes back to a character flaw in myself. I'm stuck-up. I'm "holier-than-thou." I'm "too stupid to understand simple logic.... "

Skipping Through Topics

As with other parts of their life, people with ADHD can find it hard to stay focused in an argument. Often, rather than discuss something until it is resolved, they skip from item to item. One non-ADHD spouse writes:

> Trying to stay on topic is also an exercise in extreme frustration. He'll challenge me, I'll respond, and rather than address the challenge, he'll treat my response as the challenge and either ask a rhetorical question or issue a new challenge.

If you get into this type of unproductive argument, simply step out of the pattern and circle back at another time when you can refocus the conversation on your underlying issues.

Defensiveness and Blaming

People with ADHD often have low self-esteem. This can lead to extreme defensiveness regarding anything ADHD, as well as blaming others:

> I have tried the "we're on the same team" approach and have been met with, "There's nothing wrong with me, it's your problem, you figure it out," or "If you would only...then I wouldn't have to...."

Poor Short-Term Memory

Many with ADHD have short-term memory issues due to the ways in which their brains are wired. To counteract this, put important agreements in writing, seek "brain training," and use medication, if you can. Too many non-ADHD spouses can commiserate with what this woman says:

> …in the few instances where we've reached resolution, it's entirely likely that in a week or a month or who-knows-how-long, we'll be back at the beginning because he will have forgotten the conversation.

Stimulation-Seeking Anger and Loving to Fight

Stimulation can be a form of self-medication for people with ADHD. Sometimes, that translates into picking a fight because it feels good to do so, and sometimes it just translates into enjoying the fight while it's happening. If you suspect the act of fighting has become the reason you are fighting, it can be better to respectfully agree to disagree and walk away. Or, as one man with ADHD put it:

> You both should agree [it's okay] to disagree… [because] us ADD folks love to disagree….

Instant Anger

People with ADHD can have explosive tempers, and find it difficult to either acknowledge or control anger. This has to do with brain chemistry creating an overabundance of strong emotions combined with poor impulse control "brakes."

> I feel I can't say anything about ADHD to my husband any more—if I do, he'll just blow up. Worse than that, I might venture something on a completely unrelated topic—like what I was doing that day—and he might jump all over me. I feel as if I'm walking on eggshells all the time. It's awful!

Can Anger Be Treated with Medication?

I will be the first to remind you that I am not a doctor. To fully answer this question for yourself (or your spouse), you need to visit your own doctor, who can tell you whether medication can help your specific anger issues.

That said, medication can help some people overcome some types of anger. When impulsivity or emotional hyper-arousal is a contributing factor to harmful expressions of anger, as it was in my husband's case, then medication may help a lot. As soon as he found an ADHD medication he was happy with, I also noticed that he no longer exploded at me at unexpected times. These had been very destabilizing episodes of anger because I didn't understand them and never knew when to expect them. I might look at him wrong or use an incorrect word, and suddenly I was under full-blown attack. Or not. I could never predict. I felt as if I was walking on eggshells all the time. He's still capable of getting angry, but now he does so at times when I would expect him to do so, and most of the time he simply controls the urge altogether. In his case, at least, medication helped him control impulsivity (and this shows elsewhere, not just with anger), and so helped his anger.

Medications might also help a non-ADHD spouse—for example, in the case of anger resulting from severe anxiety or anger stemming from the extreme hopelessness of depression. I experienced this for a while, and found that antidepressants did help me regain equilibrium. Again, your doctors can give you the best overall advice in this area.

The Intersection Between Anger and Denial

While willing to note their spouse's anger, many non-ADHD spouses downplay the role that their own anger plays in their marital problems. They might recognize that they are intensely angry, as I did for many years in my own relationship, but still deny that they must take charge of their anger in order to defuse it—both for their own benefit *and in order for the ADHD spouse to make progress*. This denial is the mirror image of the ADHD spouse's denial that ADHD is an issue. Not much improves until these two walls of denial are breached.

Here is a couple, for example, whose joint denial has left them both angry and unwilling to even consider negotiating their differences:

> I have been married to my husband for 20 yrs. He was diagnosed with ADHD 16 years ago. He has been on all of the medications over the years. He has decided to go off all of the medications now because he feels that they cause his blood pressure to be elevated. We have just begun therapy for the 3rd time. Everything is my fault according to him. I have ruined his life according to him. I do not eat the right foods, get enough sleep, talk the right way, etc.
>
> I have read the books, tried various techniques, made the lists, etc but 70-80% of the time nothing gets done. I asked him to go to behavior therapy over the past 16 years as well as other physicians have recommended this for help with his ADD. He refused, saying meds work but therapy would not. When I asked him the other day why he had not gone, he blamed me saying it was my fault…He feels that if nothing on the lists ever gets done then that is ok and it is my problem. I do not pester him about it. I know it is the trigger point. His temper tantrums are out of control.
>
> When I went to [couples] therapy with him the other day, he spoke for 40 [of our 50] minutes of it about my lack of support, etc.

Notice the words "I have read the books…[but] nothing gets done." She is reading the books and then expects *him* to "do." Both spouses are angry, and both are in denial that their anger is part of the problem. Anger and denial reinforce each other, raising the stakes for each person.

It can be easier to blame another or to withdraw through denial than to take the difficult step of trying to connect or to deal with your spouse when chronic anger is present. Fear of failure can complicate this for adults with ADHD, who have learned through experience that "trying harder" often isn't very successful for them. Withdrawing or denying can seem quite attractive.

Many years of anger and denial can lead to hopelessness:

> I gave up temper tantrums years ago. Anger doesn't work, and I'm tired of "dealing with it." After a long period of apathy, I've withdrawn and am starting to think that I am seriously depressed. The chronic communication issues have left me feeling hopeless. Apparently, my ADD husband thinks that his behavior doesn't affect me any more than mine affects him. He's decided that I had problems long before he ever met me and has been more low key lately, maybe he feels sorry for me. It's never a fair fight. There is no compromise. He will make sure he wins this civil war. I hate to surrender but, I don't care anymore.

We *think* it's easy to see how anger affects us. Anger is identified by yelling or harsh words, or when we feel uncharitable toward our partner. But it's more than this. Anger infuses not only your interactions, but your way of thinking—even the basic assumptions you make about your relationship and each other.

As an example, my anger at my husband colored even my most basic assumptions about what our problems were. After years of struggle and frustration, my underlying assumptions about what was wrong with my marriage looked like this:

- My husband's ADHD was the main reason everything was falling apart.
- My husband was not the competent husband I had first thought him to be. He couldn't or wouldn't hold up his end of our marital "bargain," didn't really care about my pain, and was disconnected from me and our children.
- Because he wouldn't take responsibility I was forced to be in control of pretty much everything.

- I had been trying really hard to change things. He hadn't been trying very hard at all—only getting in the way of my ideas.

If you are the non-ADHD spouse in your relationship, you may harbor a number of these assumptions. But I want you to notice a few things about them. First, everything revolved around my husband or his ADHD. Even my assertion that I had to be in control was based on my response to one of his negatives, rather than a positive of my own. Second, underlying every assumption were negative feelings about him that poisoned our every interaction. Third, there was no respect or affection in any of these assumptions; just self-pity and dislike. Not because I didn't theoretically *want* there to be warmth, but because I was so angry that there was no room for respect or affection—only anger, as well as a good dose of denial that I had anything to do with our situation. Anger colored everything, even if I wasn't aware of it.

Finding out he was having an affair with another woman inspired me to reassess *my* role in my relationship and to recognize the futility of using anger to define my feelings about him. My thoughts became:

- My husband was attractive (and competent) enough to be a treasured catch for someone else. His ADHD wasn't causing issues in that relationship—in fact, it was a plus. His openness to fun led them to many adventures, which I envied and remembered fondly from our own dating.

- He was *very* interested in and involved with her...partially due to infatuation and hyperfocus, but also because she actually gave him something positive and affectionate in which to be interested. His disconnection from me wasn't *just* ADHD.

- My feeling that he was forcing me to be in control was false. He wasn't forcing me to do anything, nor was I in control—certainly not of my husband, and even of myself. I had ceded control of my own life to lots of negatives and reactivity. It was time for me to take control of my life—immediately—and start to act like the thoughtful, loving, caring and *good* person that I was before I became so misshapen by my anger. It was likely I wouldn't end up with my husband, but I would always end up with myself, so I had better start behaving in a way that made me proud and that didn't include verbally abusing anyone or being hypercritical.

- I had been trying to change things, but only on my terms, and with little regard for my husband's real needs, feelings, or opinions. I had not made much effort to bend creatively to jointly solve our problems as partners, or consider his issues with respect. When he had pointed to my anger and rejection of him I had denied his points, just as he had denied ADHD issues. Instead of listening, I had spent lots of time dictating possible solutions or bouncing ideas off him and expecting he would like them. It was time to listen.
- My marriage was most likely over. Time to stop worrying about saving my marriage. Time to start worrying about my happiness first, and then repairing our relationship as two equals. We had children together, and would therefore be forever connected. It was time to start respecting the fact that we are both individuals who make our own decisions.

Perspective was forced on me. My anger was at least as destructive as his ADHD. I could not control anyone but myself.

The idea that we should not, and cannot, "manage" our spouse is a critical, and universal, concept for a successful marriage. Yet the vast differences between how ADHD and non-ADHD spouses live in the world, and the seeming inability of some with ADHD to do chores quickly or make financial decisions, encourage non-ADHD spouses to forget this universal truth. We delve right in, thinking we can "solve" the problem, forgetting that it is not ours to solve. Within about 24 hours this "newfound" truth allowed me to find the strength to be myself, to take care of myself, and to start *being* the warm, thoughtful, ethical, caring, listening person I had previously been, rather than the angry person I had become. With my marriage in shambles I was finally ready to focus on what I should have been attending to all along—being the best person I knew how to be and implementing the changes I could make in myself. From now on I would not choose a course of action because it would "change" my husband or teach him a lesson, but because it was the right thing to do for the person I aspired to become again.

Think back to Lerner's sentence about the inevitability of anger:

> Anger is inevitable when our lives consist of giving in and going along; when we assume responsibility for other people's feelings and reactions; when we relinquish our primary responsibility to proceed with our own growth and ensure the quality of our own lives; when we behave as if having a relationship is more important than having a self.

It is no coincidence that when I took charge of my own life again by recognizing I had neither responsibility for nor control over my husband's life, and vowing to act differently, I was also able to let go of my anger. The prerequisites for anger no longer existed in my life. This radical shift in my thinking freed me to be myself.

I had loved my husband deeply at one time, and he had loved me. We had had a good basis for a healthy relationship. But anger, denial, and ADHD misunderstandings had distorted our relationship—and each of us—beyond recognition. Crisis and the paradigm shift it encouraged allowed me to be me again. The unintended consequence of becoming me again was that my husband fell back in love with me, surprising us both. Finally, he had something, and someone, worth making all the effort for.

The Radical Shift for Couples Struggling with the ADHD Effect

Don't try harder, try differently. That's a key message I want you to remember. But what does "differently" look like? The charts on the next pages lay out the basic ideas. They revolve around the following principles:

- Respecting your individual needs and differences
- Taking responsibility for yourself, and only yourself
- Finding your own voice—that is, behaving in a way that is consistent with being the person you aspire to be and who is uniquely "you"
- Creating interactions and making choices that are "ADHD sensitive"

Assuming that you actually like each other underneath it all, if you *both* enthusiastically adopt these shifts, you will greatly increase your chances of learning to thrive again.

You may be able to radically alter your direction all at once, as I did. Or, you may take a more gradual approach. Either way, non-ADHD spouses can use the chart on the next page as a template for thinking about your relationship in a new, and healthier, way.

The ADHD Effect Paradigm Shift
Non-ADHD Spouse

The Old Way	**The New Way**
The ADHD is to blame or my spouse is to blame.	Neither of us is to blame *and* we are *both* responsible for creating change.
Medication will turn our lives around.	Good treatment has "three legs" and takes time and effort. I will be supportive and patient.
I must teach my ADHD spouse to do it better and/or compensate for all he or she cannot do.	I am never my spouse's keeper. We will respectfully negotiate how we each can contribute.
My spouse's incompetency forces me to take over everything and has stifled my life.	I am only responsible for my own personal growth and deciding what to do with *my* life.
I'm exhausted, overworked, unloved, belittled. No wonder I'm mad and cranky.	I will live and behave in a way that is consistent with the best person I aspire to be.
Lots of structure will benefit us all.	Structure helps, but patience, empathy, creativity and a good laugh are at least as important.
I have no respect for my spouse.	I respect my spouse's inherent right to make his or her own decisions and live by the consequences, whether or not I like what he or she is doing.
My spouse has little to offer.	My spouse has as much to offer as when we got married, but it's hidden right now.

Let's take a look at what the paradigm shift might look like for the ADHD spouse.

The ADHD Effect Paradigm Shift
ADHD Spouse

The Old Way	**The New Way**
I don't really understand when I might succeed or fail. I'm not sure I want to take on challenges.	My inconsistency in the past has an explanation: ADHD. Fully treating ADHD will enable greater consistency and success.
ADHD may or may not be a factor and I'm taking meds, so it's being taken care of.	Untreated and undertreated ADHD symptoms hurt my relationship much more than I realized. I will aggressively pursue all responsible paths of treatment. I'm committed to becoming the best partner I can be.
I always take life as it comes at me.	I like flexibility and may choose to take life as it comes, but better control over ADHD lets me choose to shape my destiny, too.
I am unloved/unlovable and unappreciated. My partner wants me to change who I am.	I am loved/lovable, but some of my ADHD symptoms are not. I am responsible for managing my negative symptoms.
If I just try harder, maybe this time I'll succeed.	Don't try harder, try differently. Use ADHD-sensitive strategies to make life easier.
I hate that my partner always nags me!	My partner's nagging signals inconsistency. We can change that!
My partner is the only organized person in the house. She can take care of the tough stuff.	I can create external structures to organize myself well enough so we are both happy.

You can both start working on these things immediately. The ADHD spouse, for example, can pursue full treatment *today*. Both partners can decide *today* that it's time to be responsible only for himself or herself. You can start to create a series of fun interactions *today* to remind yourself of how much your spouse has to offer.

Will you wake up tomorrow with a completely new mindset, as I did? Probably not, and quite frankly I wouldn't wish the pain of that particular experience on anyone. But keep the ADHD effect paradigm shift in your mind as a specific blueprint for how to "try differently."

Stepping Away from Anger

You might *understand* the complex issues that underpin your anger, yet still *feel* angry. You need some tools to help you let it go and overcome your anger.

> I really feel like he uses his ADHD as an excuse, says he wants to get help, but it goes nowhere, because he doesn't know what step to take next. He, of course, throws the blame on me and says that if I was nicer, that he wouldn't be as nasty of attitude…and that maybe I should get some medication. Well, if I have endured this life for this many years with little to no medication, then I hardly think I need it now.

This couple blames each other for their marital problems in a common combination. She thinks his ADHD is the problem, and he thinks she's just too mean to endure. Both are defensive. Neither seems willing to take responsibility for change. This downward spiral will only get worse if they don't interrupt it.

As Lerner points out, the good thing about a circle or spiral is that if one person steps out of the circle, the cycle if altered *by definition*. Because you are the only one who can change your own behavior, it is *your* responsibility to step out of the circle of anger.

You probably already know that this isn't easy. I tried multiple times to step out of the angry circles I had developed with my husband. "I'll just behave differently and not let him make me mad. If I do this, then he'll change his behavior, too," I would think. This approach would work for a little while, but then I would become even *more* angry that my husband wasn't really responding much. He would stop arguing with me—he didn't often initiate arguments, just responded to me when I was aggressive. But he didn't change. I, on the other hand, had been subordinating my behavior to his, with an expectation that this would get him to change. In other words, I was stepping out of the circle for the wrong reason! I was still completely connected to my husband's ADHD behavior and trying to manipulate him, rather than standing up for myself for my own reasons.

It took me a long time to understand that you put aside your anger because it is in your own best interests, not because it might induce a certain response in your spouse.

So you don't have to go through this process as blindly as I did, here are some ways to start taking control of your anger. Some of these are ideas adapted from *The Dance of Anger*, and I thank Ms. Lerner for allowing me to adapt them for couples struggling with ADHD. Again, I urge you to read her book. It is beautifully written, and provides insight in greater depth than I have the space to do here. Without a doubt it will help you as you move to de-electrify your interactions with your spouse.

Tips
Stepping Away from Anger

- **Be ready to mourn.** An important and often overlooked stage in healing your anger is mourning. You've experienced a lot of hurtful times together. To move on you need to accept that you both did the best you could do at the time and to mourn what could have been (but wasn't). Chances are very good that you both have sad feelings about this, even if you haven't admitted as much. Forgive yourselves, then vow to do better now that you know to try differently rather than try harder.

- **Differentiate feeling anger from venting.** If you think about your communications, it is highly likely that one or both of you express your anger with statements such as these (from the non-ADHD spouse):

  "Why don't you ever finish what you start?! Those shelves have been under construction for three months now!"

  "I asked you to take care of the kids today, but they missed their naps, have ice cream all over their shirts, and are now a total mess! Kids need to stick to a routine!"

  "We're going to be late again! Why can't you get dressed in less than 60 minutes?"

  "I do things for you all the time and you never do anything for me!"

  "You forgot to pay the bills again? You are so irresponsible!"

  Or statements like these from the ADHD spouse:

  "Leave me alone! All you do is nag me!"

  "You are too nitpicky for words! Why don't you just lighten up and get a life?"

  "Who *cares* if we get there on time?!"

  These comments are not a productive expression of anger. They serve only to vent frustration, demean the other spouse's behavior, and put him or her on the defensive.

- **Translate your anger into clear, nonblaming statements focused on underlying issues and validation.** Learn constructive ways to express your ideas and needs, such as learning conversations, core value negotiation, and speaking in the positive (I'll cover them in Step 4). Dig deeper.

Chances are good that what you are arguing about has to do with autonomy, fear of failure, and validation.

To emphasize the benefits of talking about your anger in clear, nonblaming statements, I would point out that expressing your anger in other ways (blaming another, changing the focal point of your argument as you go, yelling) also hurts you because it allows your point of view to be easily written off. Obviously, this is not in your best interests.

- **Stop diagnosing your spouse's ADHD**. I cannot tell you how many spouses I hear from who say "I'm pretty sure my husband has ADHD. He shows all the signs." Perhaps. But even if you are right, chances are high that there are other diagnosable issues going on as well, such as depression or anxiety. And ADHD shares symptoms with other disorders, such as bipolar and even eye-tracking disorders. It is in both of your best interests to stop "diagnosing" your spouse and urge him or her to get a full evaluation. (If he resists, point out that an evaluation does not commit him to a specific treatment such as medications. It only helps you both understand what options might be available to address the problems.)

  The comment "You must have ADHD" also sends an unintended negative message of unworthiness to your spouse that can trigger resentment and defensiveness.

  Instead of focusing on "I think you have ADHD," focus on the specific issues that you have in your relationship. If you are lonely because your spouse doesn't pay enough attention, focus on that. Once you are constructively discussing your own needs, rather than venting about them, you can plant the seed about ADHD. Do not dwell on it, for doing so will likely work against you. And you might be wrong.

After there is a diagnosis, pay attention to your partner's sensitivity about discussing ADHD. Eventually, you want to get to a point where the fact of ADHD in your relationship is neutral for both of you. Until that time, it is respectful to treat the topic with whatever sensitivity the ADHD partner suggests.

- **Take responsibility for your own anger and behavior, but don't feel responsible for your partner's**. This is important to reiterate: you cannot control your spouse's reactions to you or his actions, including anger or denial. The best path is to try to understand the response's emotional foundation better and validate those feelings as consistent with the person's internal logic and experience, then negotiate to see if you can find a truce that meets your respective needs.
- **Observe yourself carefully**. Hold yourself to high standards of behavior, regardless of your spouse's behavior. While "keeping score" is common in the ADHD relationship, it gets you nowhere. Acting consistently, ethically, and thoughtfully will help you gain confidence and feel good about yourself, even within a difficult relationship. Keeping a journal might help you reinforce thoughtful behaviors, particularly during stressful times.
- **Declare autonomy without declaring war**. Too often people assume that becoming autonomous they will no longer be connected to their spouse. "To hell with it all—I don't need him!" or "I'll just rely on my friends instead, because I can't rely on him." But autonomy does not have to mean disconnection. What you want to change with your autonomy is what you connect about. In your angry state you are most certainly connected, but about destructive things—discontent, problems, anger, incompetence, and arguments. One goal should be to be autonomous but connected, specifically around things that build your relationship—feelings and activities that are positive and meaningful.

- **Take a firm but loving stand**. This is a really hard one for most of the non-ADHD spouses I encounter. It is easier, particularly when the ADHD is undiagnosed, to acquiesce to, and compensate for, the ADHD behaviors than it is to stand firm and insist that ADHD symptoms be addressed by the ADHD spouse. Women, in particular, are taught to put themselves second and "take care" of others rather than stand firm. In addition, many women fear what might happen if they stand firm—will they end up divorced? But compensating repeatedly and sacrificing your own needs in order to keep the peace or to get things organized does not address the underlying issues between you and results only in creating frustration and anger.

  It is also hard for an ADHD spouse to take a reasonable and firm stand. It is easier to acquiesce to the partner's anger by retreating from involvement or by putting up defenses than it is to carefully think through priorities and needs and express them in a consistent and loving way. Difficulty with impulse control and hierarchical thinking exacerbates this. But easier is often not best. The ADHD spouse needs to learn how to clarify and express needs, *including the need to be valued and respected by one's spouse*. This takes effort and a willingness to engage in sometimes uncomfortable ways, something that can be hard to do for a person who may have low self-esteem or is focused on what feels good in the moment rather than what is best for the long haul.

Finding the Roots of Anger, Fear, and Denial

Overcoming anger, fear, and denial will present some of the greatest challenges you both will face. It can help to more deeply understand what lies beneath these feelings. An ADHD spouse's defensiveness may reflect feelings of insecurity about his standing in the family, for example. A non-ADHD partner's frustration about her husband's inability to complete the chores he initiates may indicate that she's concerned this means he doesn't care about her.

A good counselor *who knows about ADHD* can help you explore these issues. In addition, you can do some constructive brainstorming yourselves, providing fodder for some interesting and important conversations about your mutual needs. I have included a detailed description about how to brainstorm to get at hidden motivators in the Worksheets and Tools section at the end of the book.

Don't Let Triggers Send You Back to the Bad Old Days

It takes time to conquer chronic anger and fear of failure. Even after you are doing better, it can be easier than you might expect to fall back into old anger patterns. Often there is a specific trigger that sends you back to "the bad old days." Consider this example.

For about a year after we had repaired our marriage, my husband could be sent into an impenetrable defensive shell if I raised my voice. Yelling reminded him of all the pain he had experienced when I belittled him. The pain of those memories was so intense that his only defense was to "hide." I, too, could be "sent back," particularly if he did something that seemed to indicate that he just didn't care or wasn't listening. Once he promised me he would take care of changing my business phone service. We had a series of miscommunications around the topic—he wanted to keep my number for me in the face of opposition by the phone company, but my priority was that the service not be cut off. It was important, and I couldn't see any progress, so I nagged him about it, which had the net result that he didn't want to talk with me about the project—hence the miscommunications. As he battled for what he thought I ought to have, he ignored what I felt was most needed for my business, and my service was disconnected for a week without warning. Bad memories of all the times he had ignored me came flooding back.

Luckily, you can control your responses to trigger events. The first thing to do is to remind yourself that the bad feelings you are having don't reflect your current situation, but rather represent an emotional response to your past. Remember that humans do sometimes make mistakes and that you are both doing better. Then do the following:

- **Visualize** the trigger event as an object that is in front of you. "Grab" it with your hands and push it aside.
- **Talk** with your spouse about the trigger event. "I'm feeling really upset right now because you didn't change the phone service. But what's really making me mad is that it reminds me of the 'bad old days' and gives me knots in my stomach." (Hint to spouse: acknowledge the legitimacy of the trigger event and console your partner. Be empathetic. It's hard to relive this pain.)
- **Acknowledge** the legitimacy of your past pain, but also recognize that experiencing that pain today doesn't mean you are returning to the past, only that your past is currently "haunting" you. You are in control of your responses today and have better techniques in place to deal with the specific "trigger" problem.
- **Don't acquiesce** to the desire to blame your spouse for your response to the trigger. Instead, take actions that will help make it better for you. When my phone service was cut off, I emailed friends and business associates to tell them to call my cell phone.

When bad feelings are triggered, have faith that you can choose your responses. You'll never get rid of all anger (that would be unnatural!) but you can be secure that as a couple you've figured out the best way for the two of you to acknowledge it and handle it.

Step 3: Getting Treatment for You Both

"If you don't get help, ADD can curse you and make you wretched.
But if you work it right,
ADD can enhance your life and make you sparkle."
— Ned Hallowell

I won't review specific types of treatments for ADHD here, but there are many, and the number of research-validated options continues to grow. Check www.ADHDmarriage.com for accurate, scientifically-sound options about which you can speak with your doctor. In this chapter I will focus on the following:

- How effective treatment of ADHD is like a three-legged stool
- Why some sort of treatment is critical within the boundaries of a marriage
- Why treatment is almost always needed for both spouses
- What patterns you can expect to see in your relationship once treatment is under way

Put simply, if your relationship is in trouble, the spouse with ADHD should seek treatment *of some sort.* When people with ADHD are single, the results of untreated ADHD land primarily on them: they may lose their job, fail at a relationship, or struggle to stay organized. But the stress created is primarily their own.

Not so in a committed relationship. The declining credit rating reflects on you both, the strain of uneven responsibilities can create enormous mental and physical stress for the non-ADHD spouse, and the wrecked relationship affects both partners and their children. To ignore the need to get ADHD evaluated and treated in one way or another is an act of irresponsibility. Having ADHD isn't the end of the world. A diagnosis of ADHD is actually good news in a sense because there are many effective ways to manage ADHD symptoms. Not treating it, however, can leave a path of destruction too wide for other family members to avoid.

ADHD Won't Just Go Away

While avoidance can be an excellent way to manage many difficult issues, it doesn't do anything for ADHD, which is rooted in physiological features of the brain just as poor eyesight is rooted in physiological structure of the eyes. It is impossible to "avoid" ADHD if you have it. All a person with ADHD can do is to create a life in which the ADHD is a positive rather than a negative, or, at least, in which the ADHD is neutral.

If you have poor eyesight, you get glasses. If you have ADHD, you get *treatment*. (It would be great if the treatment for ADHD were as simple as glasses!) Treatment does *not* mean just "trying harder," just taking a pill, or expecting that things will magically change if your unrelenting non-ADHD spouse suddenly becomes an angel. Without honest-to-goodness treatment, the ADHD won't change *even if* the non-ADHD spouse is suddenly angelic; the brain remains wired as it was, and the behaviors resulting from this wiring remain the same.

Deciding Not to Treat ADHD Is Not a Neutral Act

Deciding whether to treat ADHD is the sole responsibility of the person who has it. (How to *respond* to a spouse's decision about treatment is up to the non-ADHD partner.) Unfortunately, because it seems a matter of (marital) survival, it's tempting for a non-ADHD spouse to push and push to get treatment started. This pushing almost always adds to the problem rather than helping it, as it puts the ADHD spouse on the defensive.

But the ADHD spouse needs to be aware that deciding not to treat ADHD is not a neutral act. By deciding not to address ADHD, a spouse decides that the status quo is fine. The non-ADHD partner, who has already decided that the status quo is not fine (hence the conversations about treatment) is then left with only unpleasant choices:

- Try to force the spouse to treat the ADHD (generally not possible)
- Try to force the spouse to change without treatment (also generally not possible)
- Unilaterally give up on issues that are important without benefit of the win–win potential of negotiation, often causing depression and anger
- Leave the relationship

The third point is particularly important, as it is the path that most spouses take and accounts for the non-ADHD spouse's gradual (and sometimes not-so-gradual) decline into chronic anger and resentment.

When a spouse with ADHD decides to explore serious treatment, he sends a message of hope and shows that he is invested enough in the success of the relationship to take risks to make it better, encouraging his spouse to do the same. He also signals that he knows enough about ADHD to understand that with work he can make specific improvements in functioning with ADHD. If he finds that treatment is ineffective (though some sort of treatment improves things for almost all people with ADHD), he is not committed to continue. Note, however, that *deciding* to get treatment is not the same thing as *pursuing effective treatment* until you have measurable relief from symptoms. ADHD treatment is a very active process. You don't just take a pill and wait for improvement. You experiment, measure, and experiment again and again until you find a wide variety of strategies that improve your life and effectively counter your ADHD symptoms.

Why You Both Need Treatment

While it may be obvious by now that the ADHD spouse needs treatment, it is a mistake to assume that the non-ADHD spouse does not. Treatment helps the non-ADHD spouse acknowledge the ADHD spouse's efforts to change and create a supportive environment for him or her so the marriage can thrive. Imagine that you are an ADHD spouse hounded by your partner's incessant requests. You treat your ADHD in order to manage some portion of the household chores in a satisfactory time frame. Yet your spouse continues to hold a grudge; you haven't changed "enough," or the way you choose to do things isn't "right." Have you gained anything? Has the marriage improved? Not really. You're working harder and still getting hounded. Or imagine that you are the non-ADHD spouse, and you decide to be happy and nice to your ADHD spouse all the time. The ADHD spouse changes nothing, remaining distracted, angry, or disconnected. Will you be able to sustain your happiness? Obviously not.

In any marriage affected by ADHD, the non-ADHD spouse has very real issues that must be addressed for the marriage to break out of its negative patterns. Here are just a few of the conditions that might affect the non-ADHD spouse:

- Depression
- Anxiety and fear
- Chronic stress and related physical problems
- Anger
- Behavioral issues, such as bullying
- Chronic resentment
- Negative and ineffective communication patterns
- Hopelessness or suicidal thoughts
- Self-hatred

The bottom line is that both spouses need treatment. Don't "tough it out." Seek the help of a professional who understands ADHD.

The Three-Legged Stool

Optimal treatment for an adult with ADHD in a committed relationship has three specific parts, the first two of which are true for treating ADHD all of the time, and the third of which is specific to being in a successful relationship. Because you need all three legs to optimally treat ADHD I like to think of it as a three- legged stool.

> **Leg 1: Making physical changes to your body**. ADHD is the result of specific physical features in your brain that are often most effectively addressed at the physical level. Solid Leg 1 treatment makes changing habits much easier.
>
> **Leg 2: Making behavioral (habit) changes.** Physical differences manifest themselves as symptoms and behaviors. Coping strategies developed over the years without the benefit of physical changes are usually suboptimal. Yet behavior shifts, such as creating systems to be more reliable or remember better, are what helps your relationship grow.
>
> **Leg 3: Developing strategies to use when interacting with your spouse**. These include communication strategies and creating a hierarchy of issues to attack. You can't do it all at once, so picking the most meaningful symptoms and habits to address is an important step.

To my knowledge, no one has studied the specifics of leg three, but numerous research studies have shown that combining physical and behavioral changes is better than either alone. Changing the way your brain works with Leg 1 treatments is a great start, but it's what you do with that changed brain—your behaviors—that you and your spouse will notice most. It's a common misperception that a person with ADHD can make the behavioral changes without the Leg 1 changes by "just trying harder." But that assumes that the person with the ADHD hasn't been trying all these years. Not so! In general, people with ADHD try really, really hard, but something in their wiring (lack of focus, inability to create a hierarchy, impulsivity, etc.) has gotten in their way. To succeed, they need to get the ADHD symptom out of the way so that they can then make the behavioral change.

These charts provide just a few of the treatments that can help with ADHD in each realm.

Typical "Leg 1" Treatments
Physical Changes

What	How it Works
Medication	Changes chemical balances in the brain for the duration of the medication (includes increasing levels of dopamine).
Aerobic exercise	Changes chemical balances in the brain for several hours after exercise. Induces creation of new neural pathways.
Fish oil	May improve attention in those with low Omega 3s.
Improve diet / sleep habits	Optimizes body's ability to function across all dimensions, including those affecting ADHD. Sleep improvements lessen the severity of ADHD symptoms.
Mindfulness training	Trains one to be more aware in the moment. Supports impulse control.

Typical "Leg 2" Treatments
Behavioral and Habit Changes

What	How it Works
Create a master trip packing list and print it out to use as a reminder sheet for packing for any trip.	Saves time "reinventing the wheel" and significantly decreases the chance a person with ADHD will get distracted and forget something important.
Create physical reminders, such as setting alarms and leaving notes.	Brings the task at hand out of the "not now" and back into the "now" so it is more likely to get done.
Capture ideas and things to do on your cell phone. Transfer to a reminder system at the end of the day.	Captures ideas randomly (however and whenever they come) before they can be forgotten again. Reminder system helps bring items back when needed..
Hire a housecleaner.	Compensates for ADHD disorganization by hiring "expertise."
Separate out bank accounts.	Puts an ADHD spouse with impulsive spending habits on a budget by limiting available funds. Lessens financial concerns of non-ADHD spouse, diminishing stress in the household.

Typical "Leg 3" Treatments
Interactions with Spouse

What	How it Works
Designate a time each week to jointly organize, assign and track household tasks	ADHD spouse benefits from planning expertise of partner, both clarify expectations and schedules. Acts as a reminder.
Verbal cues	Used to stop escalating disagreements. Both parties have agreed in advance to what the cue means and why it's important. This keeps the cue "neutral."
Schedule time to be together	Scheduling manages distraction for the important activity of staying connected.

Moving ahead with treatment seems so obviously beneficial to a non-ADHD spouse but often is complicated for the ADHD partner by years of repeated failures. One woman with ADHD spoke of it this way:

> I have something of an aversion to medications, which is one issue for me. But the bigger issue is that I just have this feeling that I ought to be able to do this on my own, without the help of medication. Also, I have to admit that when I take the medications (intermittently) it is a painful reminder of how incompetent I am without the crutch. Too painful, really.

The logic here, actually, is internally consistent and has to do with a poor self-image developed over many years of failure. I suggested that she think of this chemical imbalance just as she would a hormonal chemical imbalance. If a doctor told her she wasn't creating enough estrogen, for example, she would feel fine about taking medication to correct the issue and would never consider telling herself she ought to be able to create more on her own. ADHD is, among other things, a chemical imbalance. It, too, benefits from "righting" that imbalance with physiological treatments.

Prioritizing Treatment Options by Setting Target Symptoms

A partner with ADHD has lots of symptoms, by definition, otherwise that person wouldn't have the diagnosis of ADHD. It is impossible to work on all of them at once, so it makes sense to identify the most destructive one or two and set those as your target symptoms. When identifying which symptoms those might be you are looking for leverage. Which symptom, if addressed, would bring the most improvement in your lives together? As examples, you might choose distraction as your target symptom, enabling greater attention. Or perhaps impulsivity, if impulsive spending or actions are leading to financial stress.

In our household, it was impulsive anger, now recognized as

emotional dysregulation. Luckily, we discussed what the most important areas for improvement might be, and it's a good thing we did! Because my husband would have told you improving his focus was his top goal because it would improve both work and home. But for me, the walking on eggshells and unexpected anger was far more destabilizing. I could not figure out how to continue in the relationship long-term if that issue wasn't addressed. Since his job was not at risk, but his marriage was, he decided to set impulsive anger as his target symptom and, with the help of medication, was able to get it under control. This provided a stable base upon which we could then rebuild our relationship.

Contributing to a conversation about what symptoms the ADHD partner should address first can be tricky, particularly if you are in parent-child dynamics. So I recommend that non-ADHD and other-ADHD partners keep these things in mind:

- **Treatment of ADHD is the sole responsibility of the ADHD spouse.** If you are "invited" to participate by that spouse, that's great, but assess whether that invitation somehow puts you in "control." If it does, then back away and think of ways to support without controlling.
- **Applaud all progress that both of you make**. Find a positive outlet for your negative concerns through better communication techniques with your spouse or by taking them elsewhere, at least at first. Negative comments tend to be triggers for regression in the early stages of treatment.
- **It takes two partners to measure treatment success.** Often, a person with ADHD doesn't know whether treatment is working, particularly in the behavioral realm. For example, an ADHD spouse might feel more focused and find more success at work, and therefore think that the treatment is "working." But unless that focus also translates into attention paid to the non-ADHD partner (or some other important positive behavior at home), then the treatment is not working at home. And sometimes the ADHD spouse can't feel medications working, while others notice important changes. (This happens in my own household.)

- **Professional guidance can help**. Make sure to use a counselor or coach who knows ADHD well.
- **Remember that the ADHD partner may also have issues** that would benefit from being prioritized in a similar way.

How to Measure Treatment Progress

It doesn't matter what system you use to measure progress, but *what* you choose to measure and *how you define success* do matter. There are some common traps that couples fall into, particularly after they have been struggling for many years and resentment on both sides runs high.

"Goals" to avoid would be those that suggest the ADHD partner should become non-ADHD:

- Be able to do housework in the same amount of time or way as the non-ADHD spouse
- Parent the same way as the non-ADHD spouse
- Not act in spontaneous ways; always plan ahead

Goals that are sensitive to the presence of ADHD might include the following:

- Create a system that ensure the ADHD partner does *enough* housework without reminders from the non-ADHD partner, outside of the chore meeting.
- Parent in ways that are safe for the children and demonstrate enough attention so they know each spouse cares
- Put structures in place that provide follow through as promised 90% of the time. Inform partner when plans change so there are no surprises on those things that won't be completed as promised.

Regardless of the specific goals you choose to focus on, success is achieved when each spouse once again feels empathetic, loving, and safe to express feelings to the other. Within that environment, specific logistical issues can be worked out, even with ADHD in the mix.

Using a Marriage Counselor, Therapist, or Coach

Prioritizing issues and thinking through your joint goals for treatment can be a good time to seek outside help. Make sure to select books, counselors, therapists, and coaches who are ADHD savvy, or you could find yourself back in the blame game as the therapist dismisses the importance of ADHD and, effectively, the root causes of your problems.

A good counselor will help you focus on today's issues rather than on the past. This saves a lot of time and agony. Trust me when I say exploring all the pain in your past to understand what was going on just doesn't make sense. ADHD was going on. You just didn't know it then, but you do now. Yes, you need to understand the patterns that the ADHD symptoms and responses have brought into your lives so that you can forgive each other for following the paths that you did, but now your job is to determine how to move on in a completely new direction.

A good counselor will be working with you on questions like these:

- Now that you understand ADHD better, how will the ADHD spouse start to manage symptoms effectively?
- How will the non-ADHD spouse manage responses to those symptoms effectively?
- How will you overcome the natural communication barriers that exist because your brains work differently?
- How will you organize your lives more effectively to take the strengths and needs of each spouse into account?
- How will you strengthen connections and recover the love you used to feel?
- Where will your balance points be as individuals and as a couple?

If you already have a decent understanding of ADHD and how it affects you as a couple, and have moved on to trying to change specific habits, an ADHD coach can be a good choice. A good coach focuses on providing specific ADHD-sensitive tactics one can use to better manage ADHD. Many coaches will provide you with a short sample session to give you a feel for what the working relationship would be like. In addition, some will screen for readiness to change. If the ADHD partner isn't ready to commit to making substantial change, it may not be worth hiring a coach.

When it comes to ADHD, advice about specific tactics to use is always warranted, even by therapists. There is a growing body of knowledge about what works for people (and couples) affected by ADHD. You don't need to reinvent the wheel or discover these things on your own. As part of your therapy, use your coach's or counselor's knowledge about what already exists.

So how do you find someone who might help you? Ultimately, it is personal fit, but here are some things you can do to find a counselor who might best help you. A good marriage counselor will help you turn your marriage around, or at least help you feel confident you've explored every possible avenue. A good coach will help you make steady and measurable habit changes.

Tips
Finding Professional Help

- **Look for someone who knows about ADHD** by asking for referrals from others in the area who are linked into the ADHD network. Sometimes school professionals may have suggestions, as may your PCP. I also keep a list of ADHD-savvy professionals at ADHDmarriage.com and can help point you in the right direction. Once you've found a candidate or two, ask them what proportion of their practice is dedicated to ADHD to get a feel for how experienced they may be. If you choose to work with an ADHD couples coach, rather than a therapist, they will often let you interview them by phone to make sure you're comfortable with their approach.

- **Insist that your therapist provide you as a couple with direction, structure and guidelines.** While you can spend hours "clarifying" your feelings and this is one part of the process, it should be done for the sake of doing something better, rather than just understanding better. Men, in particular, come to therapy to save their marriage and solve problems, not to seek insight into themselves. A good marital therapist will take this need into account.
- **Don't go along with a therapist who seems to repeatedly beat up on one partner, or a coach whom you don't like**. The target might be the ADHD partner ("Why haven't you changed yet after you made a commitment to do so? You have narcissistic tendencies") or the non-ADHD partner ("You need to stop being so uptight and give your partner a break"). If your therapist seems to be consistently taking sides with one partner, or if your coach seems disorganized or hard to work with, it's time to find a new person.
- **Be wary of counselors eager to pass judgment or undermine your marriage**. If your therapist says things such as "Most people with your problems wouldn't stay married" or "You would be happier with someone else" that spells trouble. You may well have those doubts yourself, but it is your counselor's job to help you get past them if you can, not reinforce them. The American Association for Marriage and Family Therapy has a code of ethics that expressly forbids telling people whether they should stay married or get divorced. Yet a lot of therapists do it, particularly under the guise of helping you become happier.

- **Most important of all, look for a therapist comfortable working in the present**. My husband and I experienced many types of counselors as we searched for an answer to our marital issues. I spent a year "exploring my feelings" with a counselor with little or no effect on my relationship or my life. (But it cost lots of money, anyway!) My husband and I tried one counselor together with whom we made no progress because my husband simply didn't trust his competency. My husband talked with a different (individual) counselor who urged him to divorce me and move in with his girlfriend so he could be happy. Finally, we found a counselor wise enough to help us focus only on what we really needed for our relationship. She helped us focus on the present, under the idea that the best path forward was to let go of our past and create a new relationship with each other based on today's actions and the tomorrow we wished to share.

Finding a counselor who will help you focus on the present is particularly important for couples dealing with ADHD for these reasons:

- People with ADHD live mainly in the present (remember their "now and not now" time zones). Present-focused therapy plays to this as a strength.
- Thinking about improvements for today pulls both spouses out of the muck of their pasts. It provides a positive foundation for change rather than a negative starting point.
- The therapist reinforces the message that "You did the best you could do yesterday; now it's time to let it go." The only "resolution" to the problems created by ADHD are found in *today's* treatment of the ADHD itself (and the treatment of the other issues springing from dealing with the ADHD). Past ADHD can't be treated, only accepted. Today is when the treatment happens; today and tomorrow is when your life moves ahead.

Helping an Unwilling Spouse to Accept and Treat ADHD

It may be that your spouse (with or without ADHD) simply doesn't want to engage in your efforts to "fix" your marriage. Non-ADHD spouses frequently ask, "How do I get my partner to listen to me about our problems?" The short answer is that you can't if your spouse doesn't want to; but let me elaborate, as this is clearly an issue in many struggling marriages.

I asked my husband for his input on this one, as engaging each other in serious conversations used to be one of our biggest problems. I remember wanting desperately to talk about, and work on, the issues we had. He didn't. I hadn't understood why until I asked him, "Why do you think people with ADHD are so resistant to talking about their ADHD?" His response? "I think the person asking the question needs to look at how, and what, they are really asking."

This may seem like non-advice, but consider this: When I most wanted to engage with my husband, I pressed my points emphatically. The more desperate I got, the harder I pushed. I was desperate to solve, or at least discuss, the issues that were bringing us both such pain. Because I felt I had gotten along in the world so well before our struggles began, I thought I had many great ideas about how to fix things, *including him*. I tried to be "helpful" at every turn. When that didn't work, I nagged and pestered him. Finally, I just begged for involvement. But even in the face of my obvious misery he still didn't want to talk about "us." Every time he refused to engage me I became more frustrated and upset.

My frustration was clear in how I talked with him about talking: "Look, we've got problems here that we need to fix!" As in YOU have problems that need fixing. He knew well enough that if I thought that they were MY problems I would already have fixed them. He tried being a good sport, anyway, and we experimented in spurts and starts. We tried "being extra nice" to each other to see if things smoothed out, but since we hadn't addressed our underlying anger or his ADHD symptoms, our words were better but our underlying actions bespoke our anger in any event. I might have been nicer to him, but I was still trying to "fix" him. It came through.

We tried leaving each other alone. As you can imagine, pulling apart from each other is not an effective way to re-engage.

Long-term change can come only from within each partner. However, sometimes you can be clever about how to encourage an ADHD spouse to think about changing. Here, an ADHD man describes how his wife got him to admit he has ADHD:

> Let me preface this by emphasizing that I thought ADD was a grammar school teachers' fad-disease. There was no way I would have cooperated with anyone evaluating my kids for it, much less me. Then one day, 13 years ago (I was 44 at the time), my wife told me she thought one of my employees had ADD and suggested I read *"Driven to Distraction"* to help me better understand the situation—of course she just happened to have a copy handy. For those of you who haven't read it, there is a list of 100 questions in the middle of the book. If you answer "Yes" to a significant number of them it suggests that you'd be wise to be evaluated for ADD. As I read the questions I noticed that I answered "Yes" or "Maybe" to 85% of them and I realized I should find out more about me and ADD. I don't suggest giving JUST the questions to someone because by the time I reached the questions I had read things in the book that made ADD far less threatening to me.
>
> I think one of the main obstacles to a guy accepting himself as being ADD is that he'll perceive it as labeling him defective. Two things Dr. Hallowell said that helped soften me up were, "There are not ADD brains and normal brains; there are ADD brains and non-ADD brains." and: "People with ADD don't necessarily have an attention deficit; the rest of you have an attention surfeit."
>
> I work in a creative field and looking back, I now know that I definitely wouldn't be anywhere near as good as I am if I wasn't ADD.
>
> PS: It was never about the employee.

I love that story because it shows such a huge shift in thinking. It also reinforces what my husband was saying: "environment" is critical for getting someone engaged in thinking about ADHD. As long as a person with ADHD is being told unconsciously or otherwise that he needs to get a diagnosis because he is defective, you will get nowhere. This man's wife respected his sensitivities enough to help him "discover" ADHD on his own.

Here is the perspective from another man with ADHD who notes that working from the positive is much easier than starting from the negative. Notice his reference to what happens once he starts to argue with his wife:

> I'm the ADD spouse. Took me a very long time to face it, accept it, and start dealing with it—and I'm a guy who was going to therapy willingly. (I know plenty of guys who are totally skeptical about touchy-feely stuff like therapy and ADD, so I realize it would only be harder for them.)
>
> I think it helps us defensive ADDers to start hearing the positive messages about ADD—the work Dr. Hallowell is championing. Then, the questionnaire is very sobering for anyone who finds him/herself checking off most of the boxes....
>
> You might try approaching your spouse on this topic as you would with a kid—offer positive rewards, while also gently mentioning negative consequences, showing just how seriously important it is to you that they open their mind and just read a bit. It might sound like babying—but facing our weaknesses is in fact so frightening that we react from a child or teen state of mind, ***and the rational adult is nowhere to be found once that fight is started***. (And don't even think about telling the person that s/he is just scared!) We all have our emotionally charged topics where we just can't be fully rational.

> Imagine how a surly, defensive teen would react, and try some velvet charm (with a steel fist inside) so the person can actually feel cared for, since this is a subject area that is so fraught with shame that ADDers typically don't care for ourselves at all—we just feel bad. And defensive.

Sometimes, when it is clear that the situation is untenable for the non-ADHD spouse and the ADHD spouse remains unaware, expressing your own needs very clearly in the form of an ultimatum is all that is left:

> While I can look back to when my wife and I were dating and see signs of what the future held for me, the impact of my wife's untreated ADD wasn't clear until she lost her first big job.
>
> At that point I had been waiting for the piano to fall —the job had slowly become more and more difficult to maintain, and as it had our house, our kids, and our relationship suffered. And I knew she was "screwing up things" at the office as much as she was at home.
>
> So, despite the financial impact, I was extremely hopeful after she stopped working, and agreed to a year off to help her "regroup."
>
> Has anyone with untreated ADD ever regrouped on their own? I doubt it, and after the year at home by herself (kids in school or preschool) the mess was just bigger and all the stress was still there.
>
> This was several years ago, and despite a return to work at a much more manageable job, and older kids who could do more on their own, things still weren't changing. So I finally let my wife know that I was about done carrying the load, and while I knew that any marriage that was over 50% good was a good one, well, I was beyond half empty. And I told her it was because I still thought she had ADD (she had been diagnosed as

> a child, which made this statement easier to make) and I told her that her refusal to do anything about it was going to push me out the door one day, if not soon.
>
> Luckily, she finally heard this message, and agreed to testing and potential treatment. You see, I don't think she understood how bad it was, because she didn't have to live with her. Her feelings for me were just as rosy as when we were dating—I was even more of her hero on a daily basis. When I'd tell her I wasn't happy it was earth-shattering news, and that's how she (reacted).
>
> So she went…there was no denying it—she had ADD. She agreed to try Adderall.
>
> Three months later: Wow.
>
> While we still have some messes to clean up, and while she sometimes skips her pill and drives me crazy for a day, we're back on track to where we pictured ourselves so many years back….

To recap, there are a lot of issues facing couples who are struggling with ADHD. If you attack them all at once you will make no progress because it will be too overwhelming for you both, but particularly for the ADHD spouse. Rather, you need to set priorities, reasonable expectations for change, and an environment in which, as the man says above, "the person can actually feel cared for, since this is a subject area that is so fraught with shame."

I would suggest that the most productive way to develop these priorities and effect change in your relationship is to look deep inside yourself and find your own personal boundaries and values. It may sound counterintuitive to encourage resolution by looking after oneself, but it works when it is done empathetically.

ADHD Treatment Success Stories

There are many, many treatment success stories out there. Here are just a few. As you read them, remember that each of these people could have chosen not to treat their ADHD and would *not* have experienced the benefits that treatment provided.

> Not that meds are a fix-all, but as my ADD-boyfriend says, meds give him the clear head to be able to focus on what we non-ADDers perceive as normal, easy, every-day behaviors.... We notice a HUGE difference when he is not on meds.... In fact, when there have been the very few occasions that he has left his meds at home or when we lost a prescription a few months back, he says he feels so lost and ditzy and really does not like that lack of control. He is aware of how his thoughts and focuses can spiral out of control and can see it happening, but feels powerless to stop it.... We now have a number of systems in place that, along with his meds, work really well for us.

> Taking medications is like moving from Grand Central Station into an office where it's calmer. It takes the noise out.

> I am the ADHD spouse and...it was a totally new beginning/awakening for me realizing what this (ADHD) all entailed. I have been placed on meds and see a therapist weekly to work on my AHDH, and I am now seeing an improvement. I am pretty amazed with myself (not to toot my own horn, but hey). It was always something everyone said jokingly but it turns out it was hurting my marriage, ever so slowly.

Step 4: Improving Communication

"[Couples] are not disconnected because they have poor communication; they have poor communication because they are disconnected."

— Patricia Love and Steven Stosny,

How to Improve Your Marriage Without Talking About It

Though the title of this chapter contains the word *communication,* this is a chapter about *connection*—specifically, about tactics you can use to improve your connection as you communicate. I like to think of the connections between two partners as thousands of threads invisibly holding them together. Eventually, many threads create the "cloth" of their special ties. Every interaction, every day, is a chance to add a thread to the cloth to strengthen it, or to break a thread and weaken it.

Connection is about hearing, understanding, and empathizing. It's about sharing. And, in communication, it's about respecting the boundaries, ideas, and logic flow unique to yourself and your partner. The communication tips and techniques in this chapter will help you create more threads with a partner who is inherently very different from you.

Learning Conversations

A *learning conversation* is a structured conversation designed to give you insight into one or both partners' ideas or needs. The point of a learning conversation is not to "solve" a specific problem, but rather to understand the underlying reasons you are having trouble with an issue. A great time to use a learning conversation is when you have an ongoing problem that you can't seem to resolve. With deeper understanding and empathy it will be easier to negotiate solutions that meet both of your needs.

Learning conversations are mirroring and validation conversations. One spouse, let's say a wife with ADHD, speaks for a short while—the equivalent of one paragraph. Then her husband repeats what he thinks he heard in his own words, without adding commentary. If he has it right, then it's his turn to speak. If he hasn't gotten it quite right, she elaborates to explain what he missed, and he mirrors it back until he fully understands what she said. Then it's the husband's turn. He speaks briefly in response to his wife's original idea or question, and they reverse roles.

Here are some learning conversation "rules" to keep in mind:

- Keep your statements short and direct. Too much information slows down the process and risks losing the attention of your partner.
- When you mirror, don't just parrot back; think about the statement enough so that you can verbalize it in a new way.
- As you listen to your partner mirror what you said, make sure his words reflect your thoughts in all their subtlety. You are looking for depth of understanding, not superficial rephrasing of your words.
- Don't interrupt the speaker.
- Don't rebut until it's time to do so.
- Show respect by validating your partner's right to hold an opinion, even if you don't agree with it, and remaining civil. If anger flares, call a timeout and try again later.

- Remember that the point of using this technique is to share your thinking, not defend a position.

Here's an example of how it works, based on a conversation I listened to recently:

> *John:* I'm really upset with the latest remark you made to me. You seem to say hurtful things out of the blue all the time.
>
> *Mike (who is watching TV):* I'm watching the ball game right now. Can't this wait?
>
> *J:* You do this to me a lot, and I just can't stop thinking about this morning's comment, which was particularly hurtful. I would like to deal with it sooner rather than later.
>
> *M:* Well, maybe I shouldn't speak to you at all, then?
>
> *J:* See! That's exactly what I mean! This isn't a joke, and of course I want you to speak to me. I just want you to not blurt out hurtful things.
>
> *M (hearing the anger in John's voice and sensing a need to refocus his attention):* Oh. Well, all right. Perhaps we could try a learning conversation?
>
> *J (sits down next to Mike):* That would be great. I don't like it when you blurt things out that hurt me, which is what I originally wanted to talk about, but I would like it *even less* if you stopped talking with me. *(Waits.)*
>
> *M (mirroring in his own words):* You don't like it when I say something without thinking, but prefer my blurting things out to not talking.
>
> *J:* Yes. *(Now that the idea has been understood, it's his turn.)*
>
> *M:* But don't you realize I'm joking when I say those things? You treat them too seriously, and then I feel bad because you leave the room and I'm thinking you heard something the wrong way.
>
> *J:* I'm hearing you say it hurts you to hurt me and that I shouldn't be so concerned since they are jokes.

M: Yes. *(John understands the concept, so they switch roles again.)*

J: I don't really like it when you say I shouldn't be concerned. I don't think "intent" and "impact" are the same thing. It doesn't hurt me any less because you didn't "intend" it to hurt! If you say something hurtful, it hurts! And your apologies after the fact are usually hollow. You seem to apologize because you think I want to hear it, not because you feel it.

M: You're saying, first, that I'm not listening to you. Second, that I need to try to not say things that are wrong—that I should think twice. And you think my apologies are insincere.

J: Not quite. I'm saying you shouldn't say things that are hurtful, not wrong.

M: Okay, you're saying that, joke or not, what is hurtful hurts. But I have to tell you that my apologies aren't insincere. I really am sad that I've hurt you again. I think I'm just trying to mask my inability to filter myself, so I cover it up and say it's a joke.

J: Yes to the first; can we pursue the filter idea?

M: Yes; now that I'm thinking about this, it seems as if I'm saying my blurted-out statements are jokes when really the joke idea is covering up for the fact that I blurted something out and didn't control it well. So if I could just filter better…

J: I'm hearing you say that you want to filter better.

M: Yes.

J: But that gets me back to my original concern: if you try harder to filter better, how do you keep from filtering too much? If you could filter selectively, I'm sure you would already have done so because I know you love me and wouldn't want to hurt me with these comments.

M: You're right, I would have already done so. Hmm. Well, the first thing I can do is not use jokes as a

> "cover up" anymore. I will try to develop a habit of saying "That was my ADHD there—I apologize" and just take responsibility for it. I need to think about this for a while, so can we talk about it again in a week or so?

The conversation will go on in the future, but John and Mike have come to understand some new things about being partners and how they interact. After Mike has some time to think, they will be able to apply their new knowledge to work out how to best respond to Mike's habit of blurting things out. They will also start looking into where the hurtful thoughts are originating in the first place; there may be interactions that are inspiring the feelings he is blurting out.

You may feel that a conversation like this would be very slow, and you would be right. That's part of the point. By slowing things down in a structured way you clear the path for better understanding. Put another way: What's worse? Slowing down, or arguing about the same topics over and over again because you haven't gotten to the root causes of the conflict?

If you are an ADHD spouse with a poor memory, it will probably help you to get into the habit of writing quick notes about your findings or agreements in a journal and leave it someplace obvious like a bedside table. Every once in a while when you "happen upon it," pick it up to remind yourself what you are currently working on.

Conflict Intimacy Conversations

Learning Conversations can play a specific role in your communication. They slow the conversation so you can listen better and explore repetitive problems that are emotional and that resist resolution because what's "hidden between the lines" gets in the way. You use this conversation intermittently to address resistant issues.

A second type of conversation – the Conflict Intimacy conversation – can be useful as an everyday, better way to communicate. Adapted from work done by The Relationship Institute[12], this type of interaction is part of a larger conceptual model of how couples can 1.) better connect by understanding their own

12. therelationshipinstitute.org

feelings and 2.) practice how to express their feelings in a respectful way. Affection then builds as these two skill sets become strengthened.

The Conflict Intimacy conversation is part of this. It is a set of skills that you both practice in which the speaker focuses on sharing his or her thoughts in a non-aggressive way, while the other partner listens non-defensively.

That's not so easy when both of you are frustrated. But developing these skills is critically important because the act of speaking non-aggressively even when feeling emotional is an act of partnership and respect. The act of staying open enough to listen to what your partner is saying also shows respect and a desire to engage. Most importantly, listening to your partner and believing what he or she is saying is one of the most concrete ways to demonstrate that you both have equal status in the relationship. That's a big deal when you're getting out of parent-child dynamics!

To help develop good conflict intimacy skills it helps to keep these ideas in mind:

- **Your partner's ideas deserve respect, simply because your partner holds them.** You may not understand why your partner feels that way, and you might not agree with the idea. Neither matters. What's important is that your partner feels this way and is trying to communicate that to you. Listen well. Ask questions to clarify.

- **Your partner's opinion is just as legitimate as your own**. Further, your partner is the expert on his opinion. You aren't.

- **When your partner is talking about you, you may feel defensive.** That's natural…but the idea is to stay open. So set a verbal cue that says "Wait, I'm starting to feel defensive," with the response to that cue being for your partner to stop talking a bit and for you to calm down and open yourself back up.

- **Believe your partner.** Sometimes my husband says things that seem so unlikely to me that I don't know what to make of them. The best approach is that he knows what he is talking about because it is his experience. My job is to listen, not judge. I can ask questions if I'm curious to learn more.

- **You cannot control your partner's opinion.** And you may not be able to change it, either. But at least you can understand it, and that can provide the basis for figuring out a work around to get out of your mutual "stuck place."
- **Be really, really aware of your tone of voice.** The hardest part of this type of conversation is keeping frustration, anger and the desire to bop your partner over the head with the closest frying pan at bay. Jokes aside, your best chance at being heard is to speak in a tone of voice that your partner is capable of hearing. The fewer defensive responses that need to be calmed, the better.
- **Apologies for past actions are not required.** Consideration of opinions is.

It will take time to develop this particular skill set, and a good therapist can help you by playing the role of referee as you first start. The quick emotionality of many with ADHD adds to the challenges. That said, it's one of the most important skill sets couples can build that will support a happy relationship in which both can feel safe and heard.

The Importance of Validation

One of the reasons learning conversations work well is that they give you a chance to have some "a-ha" moments about your spouse's life and your own motives. Mike's jokes make much more sense now that Johnn understands his logic, and John's concern that Mike will withdraw from conversing is more clearly stated. Acknowledging that the logic is internally consistent, even if you disagree with the conclusion that the logic leads to, is a form of supporting your spouse and relationship called *validation*. It is important for both spouses, particularly when your relationship is in crisis. Validation is a form of sharing power. If you respect others enough to be able to see their logic and "believe" their feelings, you are bestowing stature on them in your relationship. Conversely, if you write off their ideas, you diminish them. Learning how to validate your partner's feelings, to acknowledge their reality, can go a long way toward keeping your household calmer and keeping arguments in check.

When conflict arises, there are several ways you can respond: You can de-escalate the conflict, match the conflict, or escalate the conflict. A surefire way to escalate conflict is to invalidate your partner's idea. So, if Susan says, "I really hate that you never help around the house," a defensive response such as "What are you talking about? I always help out," a sarcastic "Yes, dear," or even an "I can't deal with this" and leaving the room will escalate the conflict. Rather than acknowledging her feelings with a simple "I'm sorry you feel that way—let's talk about it," Susan's partner has tried to invalidate her point of view. This leads directly to resentment and hard feelings. Susan may or may not be right, but her *perception* is that her spouse isn't helping out and doesn't care about her opinion. The only way to deal with it effectively is to figure out what's going on (including identifying hidden emotions) and then create a plan to deal with her feelings and the situation. Otherwise she remains in limbo, unresolved and frustrated.

Non-ADHD partners invalidate their partners all the time, too. When Bill says, "I can't do X" and Linda replies, "Of course you can do X—it's so simple," she is ignoring what Bill is telling her. It is hard for a non-ADHD spouse to be empathetic with the complete sense of being overwhelmed that many with ADHD experience. This leads to a general sense that "If I can do it, so can you," rather than an acknowledgement that the ADHD partner's experience is unique and worthy of validation. A better response would have been, "I understand you can't do X right now the way you've been trying, but perhaps there is a different approach you could take?"

When I speak with clients about validation, I often hear, "But what if I don't agree with what my spouse is saying? Why should I tell her I do?" Validation isn't about agreement, or about saying the "right" words to get a partner to calm down. It's about expressing that you understand your partner's logic, even if you don't agree with it, and that each of you has the right to hold your own opinion. And if you *don't* understand the other's logic, it's time to engage in a learning conversation so you can do so.

The need for improving how you validate each other's right to be different, have different logic patterns, and be unique is so important that I suggest all couples do the Two-Day Validation Tracking Worksheet in the Worksheets and Tools section at the end of the book. You don't have to agree with each other, but validating each other's ideas is a must.

Five Core Values Can Shore Up Your Negotiations

Negotiation is part of any marriage. A particularly good approach for those with ADHD issues in their marriage is that put forward by Roger Fisher and Daniel Shapiro in their book *Beyond Reason: Using Emotions as You Negotiate*. Both authors are experts at negotiation, which they have taught at Harvard Law School. In *Beyond Reason*, they write about how to negotiate, given that emotions are powerful, always present, and hard to handle—all highly relevant factors in ADHD relationships.

The emotions that you are feeling in your relationship can be either obstacles or assets in your negotiations with your spouse, depending on whether those emotions are generally negative (obstacles) or positive (assets). But the authors point out that just telling yourself that you should shift your emotions from negative to positive, or trying to ignore emotions, are ineffective strategies for change. Those emotions are there; you can't just ignore them away. Another approach might be to "deal directly with all of your emotions," which is probably what you've been trying to do for quite some time now. But that's hard, time consuming, and exhausting. Instead, they suggest that you focus on some "core concerns" that underlie many human emotions and most of your marital negotiations. These core concerns are basic human needs, important to us all, that *stimulate* the emotions you are feeling during negotiations.

Fisher and Shapiro's negotiation framework works well with what you've been learning about ADHD. Take a look at this chart:

Five Core Concerns [13]

Core Concerns	The Concern is Ignored When...	The Concern is Met When...
Appreciation	Your thoughts, feelings, or actions are devalued.	Your thoughts, feelings, and actions are acknowledged as having merit.
Affiliation	You are treated as an adversary and kept at a distance.	You are treated as a colleague.
Autonomy	Your freedom to make decisions is impinged upon.	Others respect your freedom to decide important matters.
Status	Your relative standing is treated as inferior to that of others.	Your standing where deserved is given full recognition.
Role	Your current role and its activities are not personally fulfilling.	You so define your role and its activities that you find them fulfilling.

Appreciation is another word for validation or empathy. *Autonomy* is another way to think about setting and respecting personal boundaries. The parent–child dynamic is a form of unbalanced *status*. And, if you want to think of an unfulfilling *role,* think "household slave." I know when I first encountered this chart I was horrified to realize that I was ignoring *all five* of my husband's core concerns, and he most of mine. No wonder we weren't able to relate to each other!

You can use the core concerns to think about your relationship and about how you communicate with your partner. Are you saying things or making requests that impinge on core concerns? Are you actively searching for ways to reinforce and support your spouse's core concerns?

13. Fisher, Roger, and Shapiro, Daniel, *Beyond Reason: Using Emotions as You Negotiate,* Penguin Books, 2005, p 17.

I interviewed Shapiro, who suggests that it would be helpful for couples struggling with ADHD to think of the core concerns as both a lens and a lever. In lens mode you can use your knowledge of the core concerns as a way of understanding, thinking about, and learning about your own needs and your partner's needs. As a lever, you can use the core concerns as a system for creating change. In other words, you might say, "If I want to accomplish X, how might I use my knowledge of the core concerns (and ADHD) as a way to do that?"

He pointed out that it's hard to remember and think about five different areas, particularly in the heat of negotiation. So if you have to pick one in the middle of a conversation, he suggests that couples struggling with ADHD focus on appreciation: that is, understanding, finding merit in, and supporting your spouse's point of view. Using learning conversations or conflict intimacy conversations can be a good way to understand a point of view that is often quite foreign.

When not in the middle of a conversation, Shapiro suggests thinking about autonomy, or who is responsible for deciding what issues. A simple way to avoid conflict around issues of autonomy might be to use a simple rule: ACBD—Always Consult Before Deciding.

Shapiro also points out that ADHD traits may affect how a person works through the core concerns. Traits like living in the now and difficulty anticipating the future would certainly affect how you build affiliations. It doesn't change the need to build affiliation, only how it might be specifically pursued.

The five core concerns provide a strong structure for negotiating effectively for mutual gain. To find out more, read *Beyond Reason*. The authors devote entire chapters to how to build affiliation, appropriately respect autonomy, etc. The fact that the book was written with a business audience in mind is another plus, for it may be a more appealing read for some than your typical self-help fare.

Verbal Cues

Verbal cues are a great tool to use if you have repetitive conversations around sensitive topics that always seem to escalate or get off track. You know they are coming, but you don't know how to stop them. Developing verbal cues together can change that.

Here's an example of a situation in which using a verbal cue would be effective. This particular couple is not yet married:

> *She:* I know we wanted to go to the concert today, but it's outdoors and going to rain, so I'd rather not go.
>
> *He:* I really wanted to go, though.
>
> *She:* I know, but I'll be cold and miserable and I'm not feeling all that well in any event.
>
> *He:* We should go. We said we were going to go to the concert.

When this conversation actually happened, he continued pushing. They eventually went to the concert in the rain. She ended up in tears because she was so miserable, and he finally understood that she *really* didn't want to go and felt badly about pushing her so hard.

This pattern happens to be one that this couple goes through with some frequency. She says "no" in some way or another, and he continues to push to get what he wants. She describes his behavior as his being "like a bulldozer."

As we stopped to try to understand the behavior it became clear that his pushing was really the result of his wanting very badly to spend time with her and fearing a change in plans would ruin that. If they didn't go to the concert together, would they still spend time together?

So the couple has agreed to use a verbal cue. If he is still pushing after she says "no" twice, she will say something like, "We are getting into a bad cycle. Let's step back to see if we can figure out what's going on underneath." This cue means "We will stop arguing now and investigate." Since they are now aware of his fear that they won't be able to spend time together, that is the first thing they will assess. Perhaps there is another activity they can do that is more appropriate

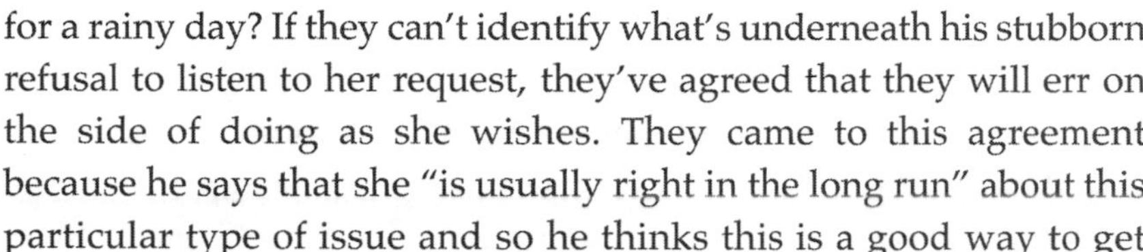

for a rainy day? If they can't identify what's underneath his stubborn refusal to listen to her request, they've agreed that they will err on the side of doing as she wishes. They came to this agreement because he says that she "is usually right in the long run" about this particular type of issue and so he thinks this is a good way to get around a stalemate.

Here's another example of a silly but effective verbal cue: "Mean Mom's back out of the glove compartment!" This happens to be a cue that my children used with me for a while. I could get cranky and mean if I had too much on my plate, which I frequently did. One day, while we were on a car trip, the kids had asked me to "Please put Mean Mom in the glove compartment." I immediately realized I was having a bad day and thought the request was hilarious. So I took the "mean" part of me and did just what they asked, making a show of shoving her into the glove compartment of the car. From then on it was a good-natured cue (always said with a smile) if George or the kids felt I could speak my mind in a nicer way.

Verbal cues are an extremely effective way to lessen the tension in your interactions. They work because they are agreed to by both partners and are specifically geared to address repetitive situations and get around defensiveness. They work because both partners agree ahead of time that invoking them is a neutral, even positive, act. Using an agreed-to verbal cue is like raising a warning flag: "I feel a bad situation developing and would like to step away from it now." Both know that stopping negative interactions before they happen supports their relationship.

Cues are great for neutralizing sensitive topics. For example, sometimes when I am speaking to my husband and feel that I'm not getting his full attention, I will say, "I'm not sure you're listening. Would you mind looking at me?" Once he has established eye contact with me instead of the website he was browsing I know I have his attention. Had we not agreed at an earlier time that this type of request was about full attention he might have interpreted the request as demeaning, or an example of parent–child bossiness. Instead, he understands it to mean, "I'm saying something important and need your full attention, no insult intended."

Cues help destigmatize ADHD symptoms. My husband's attention is sometimes fractured because of his ADHD. It's a fact. We can either ignore that fact or embrace it and work around it, creating neutral cues like those discussed as well as coping strategies that focus his attention on me when I need it the most. I'm not saying he's broken, only that I need his full attention for a moment before he goes back to what he was doing.

Fighting the "Little Voices" and Increasing Emotional Safety

Many people with ADHD have a little voice inside them that suggests that they might fail at the next thing they try to do. I personify this voice as a little devil sitting on the shoulder, asking, "Are you *sure* you want to try that?" and "What makes you think you can do that *this time* when you've failed before?"

As the stakes get higher in your relationship, and as your communication patterns get worse because your connections are weaker, that voice gets louder: "Don't blow it now—too much hangs in the balance," or, "If you try that and fail, you might end up divorced!"

Non-ADHD partners have a similar little devil whispering in their ear. For them, the destructive message is, "If you don't take care of this, then it won't get done. You have to be in charge to fix it, otherwise everything will fall apart and you'll be left alone."

These voices survive as a result of the inconsistency of the ADHD partner's rate of success. Both partners need to be aware that these voices exist in order to fight back, swatting away that little devil over and over again until his strength is sapped. The best defense against these voices is to treat the ADHD effectively and create an environment in which it is safe to communicate even around difficult ideas. The conversational techiniques in this chapter provide structures within which you can communicate safely and respectfully, even about hard topics. Here are some other ways to create an environment that is safe for you both:

Tips
Creating a Safe Communication Environment

- **Say "no" to all nagging and bullying.** Just don't do it. Find another way to communicate your need.
- **Reinforce positives.** People with ADHD often attribute their success to chance rather than intent. Remind yourselves of occasions when intent and action did, in fact, lead to success.
- **Reinforce connection by scheduling time together** when your only goal is to pay attention to each other. This ensures you get time together even if you are too busy or distracted.
- **Put strengthening your connections first, getting things done second.** The stronger and more numerous those threads are that connect you, the more easily you will be able to share your feelings and ideas. Your marriage may or may not fall apart if things don't get done. It will most certainly fall apart if you are no longer connected to each other.
- **Respect either partner's need for space** without giving up your underlying connections. I've had both ADHD and non-ADHD partners tell me that every once in a while they just need to get away from it all to regroup. Some retreat with a book; some create a special private space in their home just to relax in. This is healthy and provides strength for future interactions as long as the escape is temporary and issues eventually get addressed.
- **Organize your conversations** so that you have specific times when hard topics will be discussed. This lightens up the atmosphere for the rest of your week because the difficult subject isn't hanging over you all the time. As an example, you might set aside Sunday evening to work through what chores will get done that week and set aside time for one learning conversation about something that is bothering one of you.

- **Set aside time just to have fun and connect.** This will increase your safety net.
- **Use verbal cues** whenever necessary to redirect conversations before they become destructive. Strive to make ADHD as neutral as possible in your interactions—something to be dealt with and worked around, but not criminal or an indication that the partner is "broken."
- **Set priorities** to determine whether a topic is important enough to your well-being to pursue right then. Not every crisis has to be addressed immediately.
- **Make it okay to not "solve" all problems**. Not all problems are solvable; some conflicts come from your inherent differences. When you come across an unsolvable problem, move to the next step: creating a good workaround.
- **Say thank you.** You won't always end up agreeing, but show appreciation for participating in the process of working things out.

Acknowledging Anger and Grief

Anger, as you know, can be a significant factor in your conversations. While anger is legitimate, it is often expressed in unproductive ways that shut down both spouses.

Grief plays a less obvious but also important role in the swirl of emotions surrounding couples dealing with ADHD. Both partners grieve over what could have been, but wasn't, because of the unrecognized effect of ADHD on their lives. Even if you have known about the ADHD for a long time, you still probably didn't realize it was affecting your marriage until recently.

It is very important as you establish new communication patterns that you both recognize the validity of your grief and anger. It is sad that you have had relationship trouble that might have been avoided if you had known more about ADHD. It is sad if your spouse has struggled with ADHD since childhood and was only recently diagnosed. It's easy to be angry that life has been so much harder than you had expected it would be because ADHD is there.

My husband and I learned that an important time to either remain silent or show physical signs of empathy such as giving a hug is immediately following an expression of grief. When I say "remain silent" I don't mean "ignore." I mean stay involved with the interaction, just don't refute the statement. My husband, once he realized how therapeutic it is for me to "just talk about it," taught himself to listen without interruption, sometimes even joking, "I know, I know, women feel better just by talking!" Men in particular will benefit if they resist the urge to "problem solve" or tell their spouses how to get over the grief they are feeling. You can't solve someone's grief. Just acknowledge and empathize; don't dismiss. Over time, grief that is acknowledged and validated will heal.

The respect you show through acknowledgment and true empathy can go a long way toward helping you communicate better. You also can defuse an argument before it happens. Imagine how a non-ADHD spouse might feel in this short exchange:

> *Zena (non-ADHD spouse):* I might as well not be married—you never pay any attention to me!
>
> *Bruce (ADHD spouse):* I'm sorry that you are lonely. I do love you and want to try to spend more time with you. *(He gives her a warm hug and a kiss on the head.)*
>
> *Zena (angry, but also a bit stunned):* So why don't you spend more time with me, then?
>
> *Bruce:* You're so important to me! I guess I haven't gotten my distraction under control yet. I love you and want to do better because this hurts us both.
>
> *Zena:* You always say that you want to do better, but you don't. I hate that!
>
> *Bruce:* I'm not so fond of it, either. I want to be able to please you better and communicate my feelings better. I'm sad I haven't done so.

Notice that Bruce has not actually suggested a solution here. But because he has acknowledged his wife's anger (and its underlying grief) it's unlikely this conversation will turn into a fight. Rather, his hug and acceptance of her hurt helps connect them in a way that can serve as a starting place for both spouses to explore their issues (later, at a less emotional time) and start to figure out how to manage both their expectations and their mutual experience.

The Gender Wars and Communication

I tend to resist the notion that men and women should be treated differently, because I have too often been a victim of that thinking. Nonetheless, there are legitimate differences in how men and women communicate that are, if anything, exaggerated in relationships affected by ADHD. Specifically, there are two to keep in mind:

1. Women often find it therapeutic to "talk something out," working through their ideas out loud. Men, on the other hand, often like to "solve problems" and can feel physically uncomfortable with talking through something. Talking helps women become less upset and feel better. Talking makes men feel worse.

2. There are some who feel that men suffer from more shame than most women realize, and that women are driven by a fear of abandonment or disconnection. So when a woman expresses dissatisfaction, a man may become defensive or not want to talk about it because he feels shamed by her dissatisfaction. Women who fear disconnection and abandonment often respond to this behavior by "pursuing" the man that much more.

In their book *How to Improve Your Marriage Without Talking About It,* authors Patricia Love and Steven Stosny explore these themes and conclude that shame and fear drive behavior and communication more than many realize, mostly along gender lines. They urge readers to avoid triggering these emotions.

You can see how shame and fear of abandonment would be exaggerated in relationships affected by ADHD. An ADHD man is generally a distracted man—that is, one who is leaving his woman alone. He doesn't do this intentionally; it just happens, but her resulting anxiety (fear of abandonment) and misery are no less real. As I've noted before, to counteract the destructiveness of the distraction of an ADHD husband, you must both consciously make time to pay attention and have fun together. Connection is the "cure" for this fear.

Similarly, an angry, "helpful," or hopeless non-ADHD partner is one who frequently shames her spouse, intentionally or otherwise. "Why can't you do this?" or even "Can I help you with that?" are questions that reinforce feelings of shame about his ADHD struggles and send him into retreat.

I'm not suggesting you not talk with each other, in spite of Love and Stosny's clever title. Nor am I suggesting that these issues always line up solidly along gender lines. But be sensitive to the roles that gender, shame, and fear play. Remember that "talking things out" can be a particularly female approach to working through issues and that triggering shame is easier to do than you think, and counterproductive.

Tips
Avoid Triggering Shame and Fear in Conversations

- **Isolate difficult conversations.** If you have a lot to work through, set aside a specific time during the week to "talk about the serious stuff." This puts all the "pain" of talking into one session, rather than stretching it out, which can be a relief for you both.

- **Be aware.** If a partner retreats, the other partner should ask herself, "Did I just shame him?" and "Is he overwhelmed?" If one partner is feeling particularly abandoned, acknowledge that those feelings are real and schedule some time to do something fun or meaningful together. It's not just

ADHD and distraction; there may also be a gender issue at work.

- **Listen**. Most women do like to "talk things out" at least some of the time. A good way to approach this is to resist just delving in, but rather to "warn" her spouse of her need to verbally work through an issue. This warning serves as a verbal cue to "Please just listen and let me talk a while." Validate her feelings and right to hold those opinions, and show you understand what she has said by mirroring a few of the ideas back (learning conversations).
- **Resist problem solving.** "Talking things out" is therapeutic for most women. Don't solve the problem until you've heard the details. Use a learning conversation to delve deeply into particularly thorny issues if you need to.

Conversational Issues Related to ADHD Symptoms

Certain parts of how the ADHD spouse holds conversations are directly the result of untreated ADHD symptoms. With proper treatment, these issues can usually be resolved.

Blurting Things Out

People with untreated ADHD have a tendency to speak before they think and often say things that are considered rude either because of how they were said or their content. This is related to lack of impulse control and can be improved.

Conversations That Go Everywhere

You think you are conversing about one thing, then suddenly the person with ADHD is wildly off topic. This is a frustrating result of distraction. People with ADHD constantly receive input from all over the place; their brains are "noisy." This means that you will likely have many disjointed conversations with someone with ADHD. It may mean you also have unfinished conversations, because it can be hard to get them back on track again. Treatment that improves focus can help this.

Monologues

Where others might stop talking, people with ADHD often won't. Some of them have difficulty reading the emotional cues that others send their way if bored or troubled by a conversation. In addition, they tend to be really good at pulling lots of disparate facts together, but not so good at editing them. This can end up in some rambling (though sometimes interesting) conversations. Behavioral therapy can help manage this symptom. (But note that the non-ADHD spouses have their own version of the monologue: the "You didn't respond to me adequately so I'll say it over again, a little louder and more insistently so you pay attention" monologue.)

A Love of Arguing or an Inability to Argue

A love of stimulation leads some with ADHD to enjoy fighting. On the other end of the spectrum, some with ADHD cannot handle the stress of conflict and so retreat emotionally or physically when placed in a stressful conversation. Treatment of ADHD in general, and sometimes treatment of anger issues specifically, can help mitigate these responses.

Extreme Defensiveness

Too many years of having people tell you that you haven't reached your potential or are doing something wrong takes its toll. Some manage this by anticipating criticism and responding negatively to sensitive issues even before they hear what is being said. General treatment of ADHD and counseling can help. Establishing verbal cues interrupts conversations known to lead to defensiveness.

Poor Memory of Agreements or Incidents

Short-term memory issues can plague a person who has ADHD. Both spouses need to learn that it's not only okay, but desirable, to write down agreements and leave them in an appropriately conspicuous place. The very real upside of poor short-term memory is that people with ADHD are quick to "forgive and forget."

Relationship vs. Marriage

To me, logistical interactions are often the territory of "marriage." Who should get up with the baby? Who pays the bills? Who cleans up the kitchen? Who takes care of the kids? But to negotiate the details of the *marriage* successfully, you must first have an underlying *relationship* that is strong.

Too many struggling ADHD couples focus on the marriage details while losing track of their relationship with each other as people. They focus on tallying who is shoveling the walk, who is helping the kids with homework, or who cooks and cleans. All of these things are important over the long haul, but they cannot be the main focus of the partnership. They are logistics. And, yes, logistics are critical in keeping a family from flying apart, particularly when you have young children in the household. But the heart of your success is the special relationship between you and your spouse. Everything is rooted in your connection.

I urge you to stop thinking about saving your marriage and start thinking about improving your relationship. If you do, the rest will come more easily.

Tips

Improving Communication

- **Think relationship, not marriage.** You will be more likely to make the right conversational choices if you do so. "Relationship" focuses you on each other as people. "Marriage" is more likely to focus you on logistics, who is in "control," and, perhaps, unsatisfied dreams.

- **Protect your unique identities**. Neither spouse should be asked to give up the most important elements of who they are for their partner. If you give up the best parts of who you wish to be you will end up diminished and resentful, and the relationship will not thrive.

- **Practice validation**. It is important in all relationships, but is particularly important in ADHD relationships. Since you are so different it is important to take the time to truly understand your partner's logic and acknowledge that your partner has a right to hold a specific opinion, even if you don't agree with it. (Use a learning conversation if you're at an impasse and the topic is important.)

- **Be wary of ongoing imbalances of conversational control**. If, in your communications, one spouse is always "instructing" and the other always "learning," you are no longer acting as partners. This uneven dynamic diminishes both partners.

- **Remember to take shame and fear of failure into account.** If these emotions are present, try not to trigger them, for they will shut down the conversation. Seek professional help to overcome them.

- **Don't assume you know your partner's motivations or assumptions**. You are coming from very different points of view, so ask questions and engage in learning conversations.

- **Be responsible only for yourself**. If you are asking for changes in your partner's behavior, make sure to not cross your partner's boundaries and become responsible for that change. Also, you aren't responsible for—and can't control—your partner's response to any request you make.

- **Practice negotiating using the five core concerns**. These will help you remain empathetic and connected, as well as give you better control of emotions during your negotiations.

- **Manage impulsiveness and distraction**, as they are two ADHD traits that frequently intrude on satisfying communication. Treat them with behavioral changes (impulsiveness) and conversational cues (distraction).
- **Use learning conversations**—lots of them! Practice the technique until you feel comfortable initiating one about any topic.
- **Practice developing conflict intimacy skills**. The ability to speak non-aggressively and listen non-defensively is a huge asset in a healthy relationship.
- **Strive to create a safe environment for airing opinions and ideas.** That means being open to consider any idea, even if you've heard it before, and validating your spouse's right to hold the opinion. Strive to understand the emotional issues underlying the more superficial behavioral patterns.
- **Listen**. In interactions, the response is as important as the initial salvo. Don't just focus on how to initiate your conversation; also focus on hearing and internalizing your partner's response.

Step 5: Setting Boundaries and Finding Your Own Voices

"Success is failure turned inside out."
— Proverb

You don't need to be told that your spouse sometimes steps into your life in a way that is painful or difficult for you. In troubled ADHD relationships this happens all the time. An ADHD spouse might do such things as the following:

- Assume without asking that a non-ADHD spouse will take over key responsibilities, such as housework, chores, finances, and child rearing
- Refuse to treat ADHD symptoms, essentially controlling the non-ADHD spouse by forcing her to "take it or leave it"
- Use the personal property of others in destructive, thoughtless, or messy ways

A non-ADHD spouse might:

- Take over the ADHD partner's responsibilities, often under the assumption that he's incompetent or it's the only way to get things done

- Tell him how to live his life or try to control him
- Repeatedly try to change him (sometimes into a non-ADHD person)
- Interfere in work, personal, and health issues

Forcing yourself or your habits on a spouse without consent is what I call *ignoring personal boundaries*. If this is done infrequently or temporarily, then it can be tolerated or forgiven as a lapse in judgment. But in ADHD-affected relationships ignoring personal boundaries isn't a sometimes thing; it can be a way of life. It's done in an effort to create change or resist change, but as you already know, you can't change someone else. So how *do* you inspire change in a relationship? Do you just have to sit back and wait?

It's common to be afraid that if you try to change, your spouse will not do likewise. For the non-ADHD spouse, the nightmare is that if she "lets up" her spouse will lose all interest in addressing ADHD symptoms and obliviously continue to wreak havoc in the relationship. This fear is not unfounded; this happens all the time.

For the ADHD spouse, the nightmare is that he will gather his courage to try to make changes, only to receive messages of disappointment, hopelessness, and criticism from the spouse at the first sign of faltering. This fear is also well founded.

There are only a few ways out of this dilemma, and the one that seems to work best is to stop doing things to change your *spouse* and start doing things to change *yourself,* guided by a well-thought-out set of reasons to behave a certain way. That is, you need to set personal boundaries that are based in your core values.

Here is the more formal way I define a personal boundary:

> A personal boundary is a value, characteristic, or behavior that we absolutely must have in order to live our life, in any situation, as the person we wish to be.

Optimal expression of a personal boundary means that you can fully express yourself and that this expression contributes to making you the best person you can be. You are treasured for this characteristic and it is essential to who you are. In relationships we often moderate or negotiate how we express ourselves, even in fundamental ways, in order to live successfully with a person we love. This is a healthy part of any relationship. But there is a point at which the changed expression of that characteristic becomes so different from who you are that you are diminished or confined in a way that leaves you unhealthy. I call that point the lower threshold of the personal boundary, and in struggling ADHD relationships that threshold is frequently breached, resulting in fights for control, exhaustion, and diminishment of both partners. A picture can demonstrate how personal boundary expression varies.

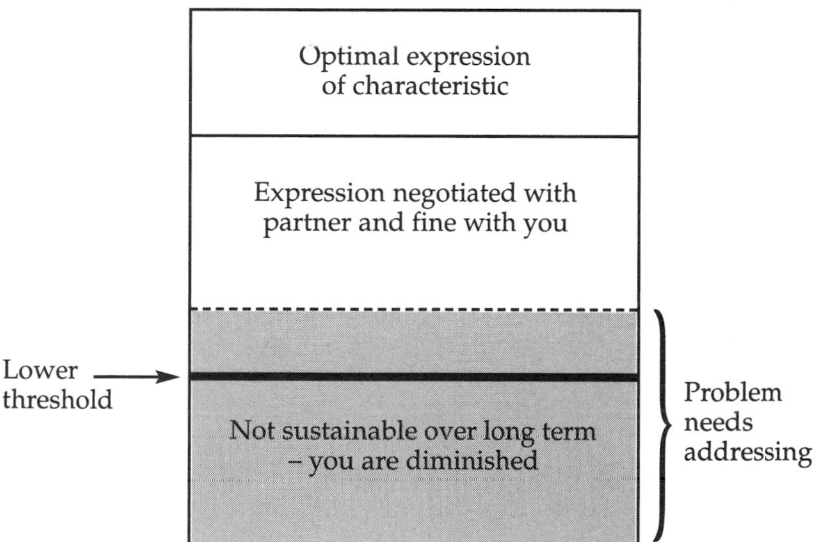

The point here is that you need to understand two things about your own personal boundaries:

1. Which ones are the most important to who you are as a person
2. Where your lower threshold is located for each boundary

Boundaries protect who you are at your most essential. When you live in a way that is consistent with your boundaries and above your lower threshold, then you are most likely to have a happy, healthy relationship. Conversely, if you must constantly suppress essential parts of yourself and live below important boundary thresholds, you feel empty, unfulfilled, and unhappy.

A core idea for improving your relationship is to define your personal boundaries and take control of your life in a way that allows you to live by those boundaries as the person you are meant to be. As you learn to respect and defend your most important personal boundaries, it is my hope that you will also learn to respect those of your partner. When couples go through this process together they move themselves along a path of self-discovery and self-definition that provides energy and strength to their union.

A caveat here. Finding your boundaries does not mean finding reasons to be inflexible or self-centered. Just the opposite: it means finding out what's really, truly important so you know better where you yourself should change or negotiate, and where you simply cannot do so. Clearly delineating your own boundaries provides the strength to be able to reach out to those you care most about without fearing that doing so will result in your own diminishment. For most people, defining boundaries means you become more flexible and more caring, not less. Well-defined boundaries allow you to put smaller issues into perspective and let go in many instances.

Brainstorming to Define Your Boundaries

Defining your boundaries is an exercise in getting back in touch with the values that make you who you are and determining how you want to act. Boundaries serve three important purposes:

1. They elucidate a set of values or priorities.
2. They allow others to clearly understand your expectations.
3. Over time, the consistency of good boundaries allows for adaptations in how you interact with others.

Consistent boundaries can create an environment in which you can live as the person you most want to be and have a more productive and happier relationship.

How do you identify your most important boundaries? What follows is an excellent exercise to go through with a counselor who can provide a good sounding board for your exploration, but you can also do it on your own. Your spouse can give you input as well. Inspirational reading, learning more about ADHD (particularly if you are the ADHD spouse), then using a journal or doodle pad can help you organize your thoughts.

Ask yourself these questions and brainstorm lots of ideas. You can hone in on key concepts and cross less important ideas out later.

1. Think about your values and what was important to you when you were happiest. How did you behave? What was unique about you? What were you proudest of? Were there important consistencies in your thinking or behavior that you can name?

2. Think about where your boundaries, or personal rules, are today. What has changed? What boundaries do you wish you had in place but you think are currently missing or being ignored by you or others?

3. Ask your spouse questions: *What parts of me did you fall in love with? How was I unique? What are my special qualities in your eyes? Which qualities make you proudest?*

4. Where do you want to be in the future?

Of all the doodles you've been scratching and the notes in your journal, can you circle just a few really important things? If not, can you create levels of importance? (Level 1 might be "absolutely necessary" while Level 2 might be "important" and Level 3 might be "could give up if I have to" or some other designation that works for you.)

One effective way to do this with the help of the spouse is to have some learning conversations around those topics in which mirroring

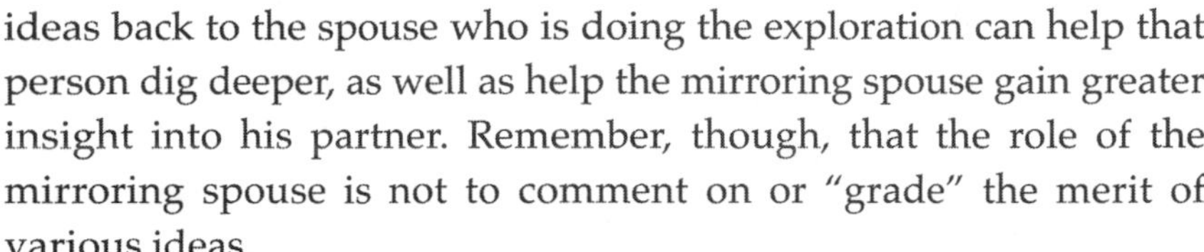

ideas back to the spouse who is doing the exploration can help that person dig deeper, as well as help the mirroring spouse gain greater insight into his partner. Remember, though, that the role of the mirroring spouse is not to comment on or "grade" the merit of various ideas.

Boundaries and Values vs. Wish List

Once you've got a potential list of values, boundaries and unique characteristics, you should examine them to determine whether they will be long-lasting and effective rules that will lead you back to yourself—who you want to be and how you want to live your life in the future. Ideally, this means separating real boundaries from a wish list of things you would like to see change. By asking yourself four questions, and being brutally honest with yourself as you answer them, you can put aside the "wish list" items or determine if they fall more broadly into a boundary area.

1. **Does the idea point back to another person?** Boundaries are for your own behavior and needs, not those of other people. "I need to live in a neat household" might be an aspect of a real boundary that has to do with calming oneself and maintaining control over thoughts and feelings. Or it might simply reflect a desire to have a spouse pitch in more often. The latter is a wish list item.

2. **Test the concept against real-life situations for consistency.** Is it an idea that remains "right" for you in all circumstances? Is it something that you feel strongly enough about that you will be able to use it to make difficult decisions?

3. **Try the idea with others.** What questions do they have about it? Do their "BS" monitors go off?

4. **Does it make you a better person?** The whole point of this exercise is to find those elements that make you the best, most "you" person possible. If a boundary doesn't connect with a core value and make you a better person, consider whether it's necessary.

In my own mind, the best boundaries

- protect and respect the autonomy and uniqueness (good and bad) of each partner,
- allow positive growth for those who seek it,
- recognize that a partnership of two is inherently different from an individual living alone, and
- are focused on people issues rather than "thing" issues.

Boundaries that are less effective seem to be those that

- are created in response to an argument,
- are intended to punish or hurt another person,
- inhibit the growth of either partner,
- do not recognize a partner's autonomy, or
- are "thing" issues such as doing more chores.

If you find that the issues that you are thinking about keep falling into the "weak" category, try to search deeper. Underneath the "thing issue" of your spouse's sloppiness, for example, may be a "people issue" of respect.

Your goal is to define overtly a few *really* important ideas that you yourself will live by *regardless of your partner's response*. Thinking about these should help you assess the consistency of your behavior as well as determine where it's important to say "No" or "This isn't acceptable" to your spouse. In my case, they helped me identify where I had been letting ADHD symptoms overrun my life, as well as areas that I could let go of because they weren't important in the big scheme of things.

When I finally got around to doing this exercise, I determined that my personal "rules to live by" (or boundaries) would be:

1. **Treat each other with respect**, even in the most difficult times.
2. **Take responsibility** for living a life that lets me express my true self, as relates to optimism, willingness to experience new things, intelligence, happiness, and honesty (the things that are most important to me personally).

3. **Let my husband express his true self** without trying to change him.
4. **Be willing to speak up, listen, negotiate, and compromise**.
5. **Create trustworthy connections:** be able to show and receive love and affection without question or deceit.

Everyone's boundaries will be different, though I suspect that many will include the concept of respect somewhere, for it is critical to good relationships. But not everyone will put "optimism" at such a premium. These boundaries work for me, though. It is through their expression that I feel I show who I am as a unique individual. Living by them gives me my unique "voice." With these ideas as a framework I have great freedom to be me while clearly communicating to others my greatest priorities.

Be critical as you try to rediscover your most important boundaries. We all have lots of things on our wish list. The difference between wish list items and true boundaries is that a wish list is what we would like, but a boundary is what we absolutely must have in order to *live our life, in any situation, as the person we wish to be.*

Your Partner's Boundaries

As you think about your own boundaries, I hope you will also start thinking about those of your spouse. See if you can start a conversation on the topic. As you become more aware of your partner's values and boundaries, keep a journal that tracks your changing thinking about how you might be violating your spouse's boundaries as well as any other thoughts you might have about your mutual behavior as it relates to your boundaries.

Once you've started thinking about boundaries you may well become more sensitive to how important actions are. A proactive approach is to make sure that your actions are consistent with your own boundaries. This will help you reinforce the importance of your boundaries. (Imagine the mixed message you would give if you demanded respect from your spouse but then did not respect her needs or opinions in return!) While this idea seems simplistic it can be harder to implement than you think, particularly if your relationship is in trouble. In my case, putting respect into my boundary list meant that I could no longer nag my husband and feel good about it. So I stopped, cold turkey. He was shocked, but it was the beginning of the repairing of our relationship. Setting this rule forced me to find more constructive ways to voice my concerns and gave him the freedom to start solving his own issues without worrying about when I would next attack.

Creating a Boundary Action Plan

Just as knowing about ADHD is only the first step to taking control of it and changing your life, so too is knowing what your boundaries are. Then you need to *act* on them.

I view identifying your most important values and creating boundaries for your own behavior as an important guidepost in a process of change, rather than a call to radically change your life. So, for example, deciding that you cannot stay in a relationship in which you are disrespected means that one of your top priorities should be to rebuild respect because it is critical to you. It doesn't mean that you should file for divorce tomorrow because there is currently no respect. (Over the long term, if you find that you cannot find ways to respect each other after working on this issue specifically, then divorce may need to be considered because you cannot sustain living under the lower threshold of an important personal boundary indefinitely.)

You've defined your personal boundaries by now, so what do you do with them? Create a plan for change, and act on it. Remember, these boundaries are *your* boundaries, so the actions in your plan will be *your* actions, not your spouse's. Again, I remind you that this doesn't mean that you disconnect from your spouse, but that you start to behave in ways that are consistent with the person you wish to be (and I'm enough of an optimist to believe that most of you want to show you care about your spouse).

Let me give you an example of an action plan by sharing with you part of my own, around the boundary of respect ("Treat each other with respect, even in the most difficult times"). To some degree

I did this in my mind, because once I reconnected with who I truly was, many of these actions came naturally. However, I did give some real thought to how to walk the walk, and this is what it would have looked like had I written it down on paper. Note that I was open with my husband about the changes I was making and why I was making them. I saw no reason to hide them, and felt that he would be more likely to understand my commitment to these changes if I was explicit, rather than let him assume that this was "just a phase." This also served the dual purpose of reinforcing my resolve to stick with my ideas. We had many years of conflict under our belts, so it still took him a while to trust that the change was permanent. I had to earn his respect and trust back, and you will, too.

Melissa's Action Plan

Respect Issue 1: Improve how I communicate

- Don't nag!!!
- Listen better, pay full attention, and repeat back to assure comprehension. Slow down our conversations.
- Don't interrupt.
- Don't lecture; share the conversation.
- Be patient.
- Change communication patterns. (Seek out good books on this!)
- Never express anger or frustration by yelling; find a better way.
- Be attentive to what time of day I approach hard topics. (Night is bad for me, morning bad for him, so weekend days might be best.)
- Be attentive to location; not in bedroom, as this seems to intensify mood swings.
- Don't belittle. Watch tone of voice.
- Try to understand and appreciate his logic and approach. Ask questions.

Respect Issue 2: Change from trying to control him into positive interactions

Cut down on negatives:

- Let him be himself, do things his way. Accept him as a unique person and stop trying to control or change him.
- Don't worry or complain when he comes to bed later; accept that that's his schedule, which is different from mine. (Give him a flashlight so lights don't go on!)
- Stop yelling and belittling—not productive and not who I want to be!

Find positives to share:

- Search for the positives; reinforce them in my own mind and verbally to him. Say "I love you" frequently.
- Look for hobbies to share and have fun with so we share more happy times together (more bike riding together).
- Make time to be together and be friends again (dates, walks, dinners with friends).
- Write self notes about positive things and post them as "reminders."
- Seek out his opinion.
- Start a daily gratitude practice

Respect Issue 3: Respect myself more for better health and well-being

- Get more exercise (get iPod to enjoy health club more).
- Work on better nutrition (fewer processed foods, more veggies).
- Lower daily stress; try different techniques—more flexible schedule, meditation, exercise—until the right mix is found.
- Start saying "no" more regularly to people who want me to do things in which I'm not that interested.

- Communicate my needs more clearly to my spouse so I increase my chances of getting them met.
- Be more involved in improving our sex life.

Notice that even when these items refer to my husband, they are still about taking care of *me*. It's not that I wasn't thinking about him, but setting your own boundaries inherently means thinking about yourself. I knew that if I could do many of these items I would start to feel better about myself and start to behave in a way that was more consistent with my basic need to give and receive respect. In so doing, I would start to like myself more, be happier, and things would naturally improve. I would at least have the satisfaction of knowing that I was living my life in line with my most basic values.

Thinking About "Me" Doesn't Mean Forgetting About "Us"

Some marriage books make a big point of saying that the couples who do the best are those who think of themselves as a *team*. I agree with this sentiment in general, but when ADHD intrudes, thinking of yourself as a team is impossible until you have clearly defined who you are as an individual. Before you can be a team you must each know not only who you are, but who your spouse is. You are so different that assumptions about each other are often wrong.

So I advise couples to find their boundaries and start living as the people they wish to be, but to make sure this does not mean abandoning their spouse. Indeed, I hope that if you are living in a way that will make yourself proud, you will be moved to act generously, kindly, and empathetically toward all around you, including your spouse, if for no other reason than that it makes you happier.

Step 6: Reigniting Romance and Having Some Fun

"Prudence keeps life safe, but does not often make it happy."
— Proverb

So many things to think about! After all the reading you've done, now's the time for FUN! Yes, you want to be able to better negotiate your household chores, make sure your children are safe, and feel financially secure. But most of all, *you want to have fun and be in love again!*

When things were in the not-so-good-but-at-least-we're-still-talking stage, my husband used to tell me he loved me, but he was no longer "in love" with me. This drove me NUTS until I deciphered what he was saying. Someone who loves another can have strong positive feelings but still not want to live with that person. Someone who is "in love" with another feels a romantic tug that pulls them toward the person strongly and satisfyingly.

I'm not talking about infatuation. I'm talking about feeling as if the person you are with is the person you would most like to be with for the next twenty years and that not having him or her beside you would be a miserable loss. About feeling genuine pleasure when your partner walks through the door half an hour late, looking completely disheveled. About having warm thoughts when you think about your spouse. *About feeling safe, and as if you've "come home" when you are with the person you love.*

If you have been struggling to hold on to your romantic feelings, you are not alone. The pressure on your relationship has likely been intense and unsettling. It is my hope that the information from this book provides new insight and concrete ideas to help you cope with the effects of ADHD. The time to move to the next step—reigniting romance—is when you start to feel renewed hope for a sustained period of time that seems reasonable to you. I can't tell you what that time frame is, for everyone's will differ; only that you should trust your gut instincts about when to take this step.

What the Research Says About Romance

A host of neuroscientists, sociologists, and psychologists are exploring questions around how we fall in love and how we stay that way. In general, it is safe to say that most couples move in a somewhat steady decline of marital happiness. One longitudinal study of over two thousand couples done by researchers from Penn State and the University of Nebraska–Lincoln showed that marital happiness fell sharply in the first ten years, then continued at a slower pace after that.[14] Even though your neighbors seem happy, for example, chances are good that they have their problems, too.

One social psychologist, Arthur Aron of Stony Brook University, has been studying the nature of longer-term romantic love, and his work is relevant for couples looking to find love again. One of the most interesting facets of his research focuses on activities that improve long-term relationships. He has discovered that just spending time together doesn't have any impact on how members of a couple feel about each other. However, doing something new and exciting together has a direct, positive impact on their mutual feelings, very quickly (the average activity in his research is around seven minutes long). Couples who did an activity that they deemed "satisfying" but not "new" saw no improvement in their feelings.

14. "Keeping Love Alive," *Wall Street Journal*, 2/8/08.

In one study he let the couple define what an "exciting" activity was. Couples chose different types of things—being outdoors together, going to a play or a class, and taking a trip were some of the more popular ones. He found that doing anything together that is both challenging and unusual for the couple helped improve their feelings.

Couples who are newly together don't get the same kind of positive response to the exciting activities. When I interviewed him, Dr. Aron hypothesized that this is because they have plenty of new things in their relationship to keep it fresh.

Other researchers have found that anxiety and depression are good predictors of marital unhappiness. This is important for couples struggling with ADHD and is one of the reasons that I say it is important that both couples get treatment. Depression and anxiety are commonly associated with ADHD—in both the person who has ADHD and the spouse, who is dealing with complex issues surrounding the relationship. If you ignore symptoms of depression or anxiety in either partner you increase the chances that your marriage will remain unhappy.

Other studies suggest that celebrating each other's successes is more powerful in improving relationships than showing support for those in trouble. Though this is not his research, Dr. Aron hypothesizes that the reason celebration works better than support is that support still has undertones of "you need my support" in it and often focuses on negatives, while celebration of success is undeniably positive. Again, this is important in ADHD relationships. A non-ADHD spouse makes choices all the time about how to respond to the challenges and changes that an ADHD spouse makes. Is it better to offer further help or to celebrate small victories? This research would suggest the latter.

All of these varied findings, as it turns out, dovetail with my own experiences. When my husband and I decided it was time to turn things around we went on a ten-day biking trip to France—something we had never done before. It was very hot, but each day was a wonderful new adventure. And, just to make sure it stayed that way, we vowed that we would do something silly every day. (I don't remember why we did this—perhaps so we could keep laughing, rather than crying!) My husband cheered on my efforts and sometimes helped me up the hills. That trip marked the beginning of our new relationship...and not just because it was new and exciting (though that seems to have helped) but because at the same time that we were having fun exploring together we had also made a vow to set aside our differences, forgive our past, and be gentle with each other. It was a winning combination.

Most important, I stopped trying to control my husband's life and trying to change him. I let him be him and gave up trying to force him to be another way. He would either work with me to figure out how we could be better together, or he wouldn't. I was responsible only for me. He immediately responded to my lifting of the rules and demands in a very positive way—determining that since I wasn't going to dictate how he should behave he could now make choices that he was enthusiastic about for his own sake. Because they were *his* choices, he was more inspired to make them work for us both.

Don't stumble into these techniques the way that I did. Find what's new and exciting for you, let your spouse be responsible for who he or she is, and go for it!

Tips
Finding What Works in Love

The "new and exciting" task that Dr. Aron first used in his experiments consisted of having couples tie their ankles and wrists to each other, then figure out how to roll a foam cylinder across a mat and back in seven minutes. Your activities don't have to be extensive or lengthy—just new, challenging, and fun. Here are some tips for discovering these activities:

- **Allow yourselves to be silly.** Even if you never found it fun to do the egg toss or the three-legged sack race, you can assume that there are some fun and silly things out there that you might enjoy doing together. Go to an amusement park and ride the roller coaster or the Ferris wheel. Get dressed up for Halloween. Join your six-year-old in a three-way silly string war (in the yard, of course!).

- **Use this as an opportunity to explore new things together.** Learn how to drive a truck, join the local orienteering group, try whitewater rafting, take clarinet lessons together. If there is something you've always wanted to do but have never had the chance, now's the time. Look up times and locations for events and clubs. Let yourselves splurge, and tell yourselves that it's in the best interest of your relationship (provided, of course, you can afford it).

- **Take up a spouse's favorite sport.** You may feel as if your husband's addiction to golf is hindering your relationship. But what happens if you try it? I know many men who would be delighted if their spouse shared their passion for their favorite sport. Perhaps it's as simple as going to some football or soccer games together. My enthusiastic adoption of my husband's primary passion (long-distance bike riding) has not only provided us with an important shared weekend activity (and lots of time to connect as we ride around) but also has had an impact on our retirement dreams, which now include riding around the country or the world. It has even improved our sex life as I'm in better shape, which he appreciates.

- **Travel.** In the search for "new," nothing beats traveling together. Plus, travel takes you away from the piles of chores and conflicts at home. Remember, it doesn't have to be an exotic trip, just new and fun. Go visit Amish country or a lake region near you. Stay in a tent or a hotel. Rent kayaks. Eat cheese and bread on the beach while you admire the stars, or go to a fancy restaurant. Whatever way you like best, get out and explore! (Hint: Kids can be fun, but don't always take them along. You need time to focus on just the two of you to renew your special "adult" connections.)

- **Stay active**. While doing the crossword puzzle can be challenging and fun, over the long haul you will want to pick some activities that keep you active. Activity is particularly important for people with ADHD; in general they need to move around. Exercise and activity will put you both in a better mood for physiological reasons, and you may well find that the ADHD spouse focuses better when active, too.

- **Try something really creative together.** Creativity is a great way to focus energy. Try a drawing, cartooning, or pottery class. Consider taking a cooking class or signing up for tango lessons.

- **Let the Internet fuel your dreams.** While you don't want to get stuck online, the Internet can provide lots of great ideas for fun activities. My husband spends quite a bit of time online now planning bike trips. This is fine by me—I still reap the benefits of his planning, and it gives him something positive to dream about.

- **Take the opportunity to make new friends**. Joining a cooking club, taking tango lessons, or training for your first century bike ride with the local Alzheimer's awareness fundraising team can be great ways to make new friends together.

- **Get a babysitter—often!** Let's face it—it's hard to focus on each other when the kids are hanging on your leg demanding attention. While some parents worry that their children will feel ignored if they are out for a weekend or on a date each week, I promise you the strengthened relationship you will gain from the connections you make with each other will benefit them enormously. If you can't afford a sitter, make a reciprocal arrangement with friends: you take my kids one night and I'll take yours another.

- **Remember to laugh**. There is no doubt that some of the things that you will try will be a miserable failure. Don't dwell on that part; dwell on the fact that you are trying new things, and laugh at yourselves. Yes, even in the bedroom! Make it okay to "fail" and you never really will.

- **Revel in spontaneity**. Planning is one way to maintain control in a household with ADHD. But sometimes it's fun to be spontaneous. Embrace that, and you can build on a natural ADHD trait.
- **Remind each other of your fun times together.** Posting photos of your adventures on the fridge can remind you of the good times when you are dealing with something difficult.

Love and Sex

If your relationship is in trouble, chances are good that your sex life is *really* in trouble. I can't tell you the number of stories I've heard from people about being asked to sleep on the couch *for years*, having sex once or twice a year, or simply feeling as if there is no time for sex. I also hear lots of stories about pornography use, and partners who want to have sex all the time.

Some of your sex issues are likely related directly to ADHD symptoms, the classic example being the ADHD spouse who gets so distracted that he or she never seems to be available for sex or able to sustain it.

> My partner has ADD and we have what I feel is an excellent relationship—we communicate well and each try our best to cope with problems/issues as they arise. One issue I'm really having difficulty with is our sex life. Almost every time we have sex, he gets distracted, loses interest, gets it back again, repeats, and eventually gives up on reaching orgasm. He doesn't have any lack of interest in having sex, and we have a very loving and passionate relationship. The issue is just his inability to climax due to his mind wandering and then after a while he just gets frustrated and doesn't want to try anymore (and often a lot of time has passed from when we began, and we just simply can't go on anymore). I admit that sometimes I feel inadequate—that I can't hold his attention—but I also know that isn't the problem.

Once you understand that the symptom distraction is the core issue, things can change dramatically. This next post was written in response to the one above:

> THIS IS ME!!!!!!
>
> My husband thought I didn't love him anymore. I wanted sex…but it wasn't fun because my mind was inundated with CRAP that meant nothing. So, I avoided it.
>
> I had no idea it was ADD. Got diagnosed, got meds…now, we keep it novel. Never the same thing twice in a row. Different room, different position, different mood, sensual, dirty talking, text msgs, you name it. And it is awesomely better for us both. I don't feel so frustrated that he's aroused and I'm not even starting to heat up yet. I hated that! Or there was a noise, the dog moved, etc. etc. etc. that would simply render me so distracted that I was done.
>
> Granted, it's much easier when we have daytime opportunity cuz the meds help a LOT! But being able to stick to my diet and losing 10lbs in the last 5 weeks has helped my view of myself greatly. It's hard to think that someone wants you or thinks you are sexy when all you focus on is the things you don't like. Working on some other self esteem issues has helped as well.
>
> It's not a cure. I'm not perfect—and never will be. But, I can say this—our sex life is important and we weren't treating it that way and it suffered even more drastically because of my ADD. It is more important than dirty dishes or watching tv…and when we treat it that way, it really is a good thing.

Another version of how distraction affects sex is that you just never seem to find time to get together. This means, as unromantic as it sounds, you need to schedule some time for sex. If that bothers you, my only advice is that you need to forgive that aspect of your ADHD spouse's way of being. You can either solve the problem by scheduling sex together, or you can create a bigger problem by waiting around for a frequently distracted spouse to think about sex at a time that works for both of you. As this won't happen very often, this approach sets you both up for failure and unhappiness.

Without going deeply into sexual issues and ADHD, here are a few things to be aware of:

- **Keep your sex life varied** to help the ADHD partner remain interested.
- **Distraction in the ADHD partner doesn't mean a non-ADHD partner is unattractive.** Talk about and work through ways to communicate your desirability to each other. Don't expect either partner to "guess."
- **Find ways to show each other you care**. Romance and connection are critically important. Some ADHD partners may benefit from creating audible or visual reminders to let their spouses know how they feel—perhaps a calendar reminder to write a quick email once a day, for example.
- **Pornography use** can be a form of self-medication (stimulates dopamine production in the brain), but it can ruin a couple's sex life if it replaces regular sex or repulses the other partner. Seek professional help if you get embroiled in fights over porn.
- **Lower sex drive**. Some research indicates that at least some people with ADHD experience less interest in sex, but the research does not delve into why.
- **Higher sex drive.** On the other hand, some with ADHD find they need sex multiple times a day.
- **Parent–child dynamics will kill your sex life fast**. So will nagging. Stay away from both.
- **Ask your spouse if sex feels like a "chore."** If the answer is yes, then your relationship is probably out of balance. Seek counseling to get at the issues that are keeping you apart.

If you are currently having sexual issues, you are not alone. I suggest you start addressing them slowly so as not to compound them. Start by snuggling on the couch when you are watching television, or holding hands while you take a walk in the woods. Perhaps you can wash her hair or give him a massage. Creating these personal but nonthreatening connections can communicate in a meaningful way, "I want to be with you." So don't "wait" for your spouse to tell you what they want from you—ask.

Find ways to hug or touch your spouse for a moment, "just because," to remind her that you are thinking of her. One of my favorites in this category is kissing my husband on the head when he is at his computer in our kitchen. I like the feel of his short, fuzzy hair, and he likes that I'm thinking of him.

One great way to jump-start intimacy is to agree to set aside ten minutes at the beginning or the end of day just to cuddle in bed. Agree that this is not for sexual initiation, just for cuddling and improving your connection. Saying nice things to each other, such as "I like how warm you are" or "You did a nice thing for me today when you took my car to be washed—thank you," can be simple ways to reinforce the positive. Sometimes, just listening to a heartbeat can be a positive experience. At the point in our relationship in which our intimacy had broken down, my husband and I agreed to schedule this cuddle time every morning for a number of months, setting our clocks ten minutes earlier in the morning. And it really did help start our days on a positive note. I highly recommend it!

I hear from many couples that one of their intimacy issues is the time that each partner goes to bed. It's common that an ADHD spouse's biological clock keeps him up late into the night, while his exhausted spouse goes to bed early. As a result, they each miss the satisfaction that touching each other can bring, even without sex. If this is the case in your household, consider spending time together cuddling when the first spouse normally goes to bed. After that partner is asleep, the night owl can get back out of bed for a while longer before returning to sleep, or can read with a night light or surf the Internet in bed on his laptop. This time together is critically important to the two of you as a couple, and needs to become a priority so that you can begin to accrue positive feelings to offset the negatives you encounter.

As your relationship starts to thaw out, you should be able to use some of what you've learned about newness and romance to reinforce your connections. I'll let you use your imagination to apply the concepts "new" and "challenging" to your sex life.

Forgiveness goes a long way toward improving your sex life, too. It's virtually impossible to have a good sexual experience if you are angry or resentful. If negative feelings are getting in your way, I suggest reading *Dare to Forgive* by Ned Hallowell to find out why forgiving your spouse is a gift you give yourself. There is no brighter example of this than in the sexual arena.

The bottom line on using sex as part of reigniting romance is connection. As you work through all of the other issues discussed in this book, the opportunities for your sex life will improve. Healthy, happy sex may be the last thing to come back, but if you start slowly and focus on warming up your connections it will come (pun intended).

All You Need Is Attention

"All you need is love," the Beatles sang. An entire generation grew up singing the lyrics to that song. If we just love someone enough, everything will turn out right and we'll find true romance. Baloney! True romance is all about mindful *attention,* which is why it's such a potentially thorny issue for couples dealing with ADHD.

For those of you with ADHD: If you focus on only *one thing* that will improve your relationship once your symptoms are under better control, focus on paying attention to your spouse. I don't mean the "obeying your spouse" sort of attention, which can lead to an imbalance of power in the relationship. I mean *attending to* your partner. Do whatever you need to do to pay attention so she knows she is special. If you are out of the house working very long hours, schedule time with her, or even consider finding a different job. If distractibility is keeping you from getting into bed, set up a structure such as an alarm that changes that. Write yourself notes. A sticky note on your mirror that says "Pay Attention!" may remind you to give your spouse a hug and a kiss in the morning. Or write your spouse notes each evening as you brush your teeth (leave a pad of Post-it notes next to your sink with a pen—it takes 30 seconds to scratch an "I love you" and post it where your spouse will see it).

Set that early alarm to cuddle, even if it leaves you a bit groggy. (That's what coffee is for!) Set aside money so you can take a trip together. (Make a chart to follow your progress if you need a visual reminder to save.) And ask for your spouse's input and ideas: "How could I pay attention to you in a way that is meaningful?" It's a legitimate and important question to ask. If her answer seems odd or unromantic, like mine was ("By taking over the evening dishwashing"), find out why she feels this way; it may give you some helpful insights into her life. If she continues to feel that this is the most important way you can show her you love her, start washing dishes. My husband did. After he stopped grumbling, he realized that it made me happy enough that he reaped real benefits.

The hardest possible thing for a person with ADHD to do is to pay attention. This makes it all the greater a gift when an ADHD spouse figures out how to consistently bestow attention. Hard as it may be, you can do it if you set systems in place to help you. There's no embarrassment in this! You are simply taking responsibility for nurturing your marriage. If you need to set an alarm to pay attention regularly because your brain works a certain way, so be it! Your marriage hinges on your taking responsibility for making your spouse feel attended to. If you don't put special effort into this particular aspect of your relationship, you will end up without a relationship. Paying attention in order to keep things humming may not sound romantic, and it probably does sound like a lot of work. But you can gain immediate gratification each time you hold your spouse's hand and she smiles back at you. How many other (healthy) ways can you think of to get such consistent immediate gratification *and* build long-term benefit? Your mindful attention will keep you connected to each other, which is at the heart of every successful relationship.

For the non-ADHD spouse: Romance with an ADHD spouse

comes in unexpected ways. It's not likely that your spouse will be good at regularly planning special dates (or even arriving on time for the dates *you* plan). Let go of your dreams that your husband will whisk you off your feet to do fun things every week and let the good planner in the family plan without worrying about "roles."

Your ADHD partner may do lots of heartwarming things that you won't expect—perhaps things that you didn't necessarily anticipate or even want. My husband has "modified" my bike so many times in eager anticipation of how much it will improve my riding experience that I finally had to say, "Stop! *Please* ask me before you change something!" But I have to smile. He is thinking about me, and he is doing things that he thinks I'll appreciate. If he doesn't always hit the mark that's okay…I don't always hit the mark with him, either, and when I miss he's unfailingly polite about it. (And, truth be told, the modifications he makes do improve my experience.) Other times he'll plan every detail of a complex vacation (love that hyperfocus!) that is simply perfect. His gift is a trip that is "just right."

Romantic love is an ongoing series of gifts given simply because you want to give. This is quite different from the "I'm giving this to you because I think it will help you change" kind of gift. And different again from the "I don't like you enough to want to give you any gifts—I'm too tired to give more, and you haven't given me anything lately" attitude of the worn-out spouse or partner.

As you think about what "gifts" you can give, focus on:

Connection—any activity that builds your friendship and provides ample opportunity for fun back and forth, as well as any activity that improves your knowledge of each other's positive attributes.

Rejuvenation—trips, massages, exercise, immersion in the creative (literature, music, art, cooking, etc.), and working for a cause all have the power to rejuvenate people. Connect around creating something special together.

Being heard—sometimes the most romantic thing you can do for someone is the thing you least want yourself, but your spouse is wild about. I know one couple that regularly "exchanges" gifts of this type. He goes to the opera with her (though he's not very fond of it) and she goes to shoot-'em-up action films with him (ditto). Doing the dishes probably fits into this category, too.

Feeling beloved—the most romantic thing you can do for people is to make them feel loved and important in your life. Picking activities that reinforce how cherished someone is to you will help you improve your connections to each other. This is one of the reasons the "cuddle in the morning" exercise works; a couple's commitment to this time reinforces the positive in audible and tactile ways, and says, "You're important to me."

The Hardest Work of Falling in Love Again: Rebuilding Trust

I used to call my husband "consistently inconsistent." The only thing I could trust was that I had no idea what he would do next, other than that it probably was not what I wanted him to do. If you are married to a person with ADHD whom you no longer trust, you know exactly what I mean.

One issue with rebuilding trust when ADHD is in the picture is that there will always be some inconsistency in the ADHD partner's performance. This means trust cannot be based on whether or not an ADHD partner always follows through. Instead, it needs to be based upon evidence that the partner is managing ADHD to the best or his or her ability combined with good communication and a healthy dose of loving affection.

Trust takes time. As the commercial used to say, you "earn it… the old-fashioned way." Rebuilding trust that has been broken also takes dealing with your past. People do this in different and very personal ways. One method is a sort of "forgive and forget." You can't really forget, but you can deal adequately with your past hurts. For this to be effective, you must keep in mind that the objective isn't to relive the past or to "fix" it, but to validate and accept it for the benefit that it provides *today*. You didn't know ADHD was there, but the memories of the cruel comment one partner made to the other live on. Let that partner talk about his or her feelings. Don't refute them or try to explain them. Just listen, then show with hugs or words that you understand. It is the acknowledgment and repair activities that make this approach work.

Not letting anger and frustration from past experiences hold you hostage can clear a path for creating something new. But what will that new thing be? If you are trying to develop a more trusting relationship, it had better include some changes in behavior, or the past will repeat itself and become your new present. So "forgive and forget" is always predicated on better treatment of ADHD, and treatment and changes for the non-ADHD spouse as well.

I also happen to like "trust but verify" as a way of reassuring yourself that a spouse who has had trouble being honest or has been terribly inconsistent is changing his or her ways. I used this one to determine, after one false start, that my husband was no longer continuing his affair. Part of our agreement about staying together was that I would contact his ex-girlfriend sometime in the following twelve months to verify that they were no longer an item. If I found out otherwise, then there would be no discussion, just divorce papers. Sound businesslike? Sure, but I deserved to know he could keep his word. And he deserved to have a system in place that would allow me to trust him enough on a daily basis that we could move forward with our lives without my constantly wondering if he was lying. We both knew exactly what was at stake and what the time frame was. Even though things seemed to be going well, I did make that contact simply because I had promised myself I would.

The reason that "trust but verify" works is that it sets specific standards to which your spouse knows he or she will be held. But make sure that you use this only for really important issues; if you find that your spouse is still doing the unwanted activity you may need to act on your promised response. Do you want to divorce over whether he's joining his buddies at the bar on Friday night? Maybe not. And beware. Issues that include addictive behaviors, such as pornography use, drinking, drugs, and sex addiction, require professional intervention and time in order to be resolved. Setting a high bar without getting intervention and giving each other enough time to change your habits ensures failure.

Rebuilding trust takes thoughtful and honest communication and a specific set of agreements about what each of you needs. It takes the ability to prioritize, which is where understanding your own boundaries and who you are when you are at your best is important. It also takes healthy doses of empathy and realism. Remember that ADHD is not an issue of weak willpower, nor an issue of simply "fixing" ADHD symptoms. It takes time to change ingrained habits and ineffective coping strategies *being used by both partners*. And some symptoms may never go away, in which case it takes time to create a satisfactory workaround. Set realistic and reasonable goals, and measure how effectively you are working toward them. If your trust is based on whether your ADHD wife will *always* be able to think ahead and anticipate, or whether your non-ADHD husband will *never* raise his voice, you will set yourselves up for failure. Some day she won't anticipate a looming problem that was obvious to you, or he will lose his cool. Maybe tomorrow.

Reestablishing trust means reestablishing connections and changing your communication patterns. It means accepting (trusting) that life will continue to remain unpredictable, and that has a lot to do with both life and ADHD.

In my mind, the best sort of trust comes from agreeing that no one is perfect but we can consistently try to nurture a happy life together. We will work, every day, to strengthen our connections *and make sure our lives are organized in a way that lets us bestow the gift of attention*. This trust is based on reinventing the friendship in a marriage—or, in our case, discarding our "old marriage" and replacing it with our "new marriage."

All of this relies on understanding and managing ADHD symptoms effectively, honing our acceptance and forgiveness skills, and respecting our individual needs.

Over time, your joint efforts can result in a thriving relationship. If you are like my husband and me, you will find your marriage strengthened by the path you have traveled together, your bonds deeper and more meaningful, your respect for the sacrifices each partner has made and the ground each has covered increased to a point of awe. You will not question whether you are significant to your partner. You will know that you are because of the journey you have taken together…and you will trust your renewed love.

Epilogue: Don't Try Harder, Try Differently (and Other Important Ideas)

The ADHD Effect on Marriage is jam-packed with new ways to think about how to create the marriage you've always wanted in spite of the presence of ADHD. For easy reference, here are some of the critical points, in order of importance:

1. **Get treatment**. This is required not just for the ADHD, but for non-ADHD spouse issues, as well. Without treatment, you won't make the significant progress you seek. Think of treatment as a three-legged stool: **physical changes** such as medication and exercise, *plus* **behavioral (habit) changes** that create systems for getting around ADHD symptoms, *plus* **developing constructive ways to interact with each other**.
2. **Remember that you are not the same**. ADHD and non-ADHD spouses are really different! Use learning conversations to understand your spouse's "way of being." Stop assuming you can anticipate how your spouse will react to you or your ideas.
3. **Understand your personal values and boundaries and stick to them.** Make sure you and your spouse understand each other's "minimum requirements" for a healthy relationship. These boundaries help you and others understand who you

are in your relationship. Good, thoughtfully defined boundaries help you to feel good about your relationship even when your marriage is hard.

4. **Leave responsibility for ADHD symptom management with the ADHD spouse**. Otherwise, your relationship becomes unbalanced, with the non-ADHD partner holding all responsibility, and the ADHD partner very little. Avoid at all costs parent–child dynamics and chronic nagging.
5. **Take emotional dysregulation seriously**. Impulsive anger and strong reactions easily destabilize a relationship.
6. **Don't try harder, try differently**. Create routines and approaches that acknowledge the existence of ADHD in your lives in a neutral (ADHD-sensitive) way. Verbal cues and organizational structures are just some of the smart ways you can manage ADHD so that it no longer controls your lives.
7. **Eradicate the blame game from your relationship**. ou are both responsible for your problems, and have both played a part in a complex action–reaction cycle. Take responsibility only for your own role in your relationship.
8. **Step out of the cycle of anger.** Chronic anger harms your relationship. Interrupt your exchanges of anger by stepping away from them and approaching your issues from a new direction. Look deeper for the significance of your arguments.
9. **Reestablish connection**. Think "relationship" rather than "marriage," and think every day about creating thousands of threads that will connect you together. People are more important than logistics.
10. **Be aware of shame and fear.** Shame about underachievement and fear of abandonment often paralyze couples. You must acknowledge the power of these feelings to create effective ways to overcome them.

11. **Use the specific conversational techniques in this book**. Learning conversations, conflict intimacy conversations, verbal cues, and negotiating using the five core concerns are all ADHD sensitive and will help you connect.

12. **Tackle the chore wars with the Recipe for Success system**. Used consistently, it can (almost) end conflict over household tasks. Find it in the Tools and Worksheets section.

13. **Give each other the gift of attention**. It's important to communicate in as many ways as possible that your partner matters to you. Don't forget validation as an important form of attention and respect. Seek ways to validate your spouse's point of view, even if you don't agree with it.
14. **Have fun and laugh together.** Laughter heals, and life is never predictable. Learn to appreciate what you have today by enjoying what you can. Make sure to include challenging and new activities in your lives to build connection.
15. **Seek help from people who understand ADHD**. Get medical treatment for both spouses. Get help with logistics, too (housekeeping, accounting, babysitting, professional training). Not only do you not have to do this alone, you shouldn't try to.
16. **Remember that change takes time**. You both have a history of coping in certain ways. It takes time to identify those problems you wish to change, create a safe environment, and find enough success to rebuild trust. Don't let your initial excitement about starting treatment, and then corresponding disappointment that things don't change right away, discourage you.
17. ***Applaud your progress!*** Remember that celebrating successes is much more rewarding than "helping out." Take pleasure in the small "wins" and you will find that they snowball into something bigger and better. Not everything you attempt will work, and laughing at those that don't (or finding some small part of your effort that *did* work) will help you move on. There is much to do, and much to be thankful for, too.

Worksheets and Tools

Chore Score Worksheet

Track your chores for a week. At the end of each day take 5 to 10 minutes to capture that day's chores; you'll have trouble remembering them accurately if you leave it longer. Record your tasks using a worksheet like the example below. Assign each chore a likability rating and a difficulty rating. (Note that these ratings are your opinion only. You will likely rate the same chores differently.)

At the end of the week, sit down and compare your chore charts. How do your efforts compare? Is one spouse doing all the "fun" stuff? Are the hours you are putting in balanced? Use these sheets as a starting place for developing a more satisfying distribution of effort based on your personal preferences, strengths, and weaknesses.

My Chore Score Worksheet

Chore	Time Spent	Likability Rating	Difficulty Rating

Likability Rating:
1 = I like doing this
2 = I don't mind doing this
3 = I dislike doing this
4 = I hate doing this

Difficulty Rating:
1 = Very easy *(mindless or simple)*
2 = Moderate *(takes some planning and/or time)*
3 = Fairly difficult *(somewhat strenuous, more planning, a good challenge)*
4 = Very difficult *(physically strenuous, many complex steps, new, challenging)*

Recipe for Success

Here's a great idea for organizing and assigning chores that my clients love. Get a recipe box and fill it with 3 x 5 cards. Create five sections in the box: This Week; Later; To Discuss; Done; Blanks.

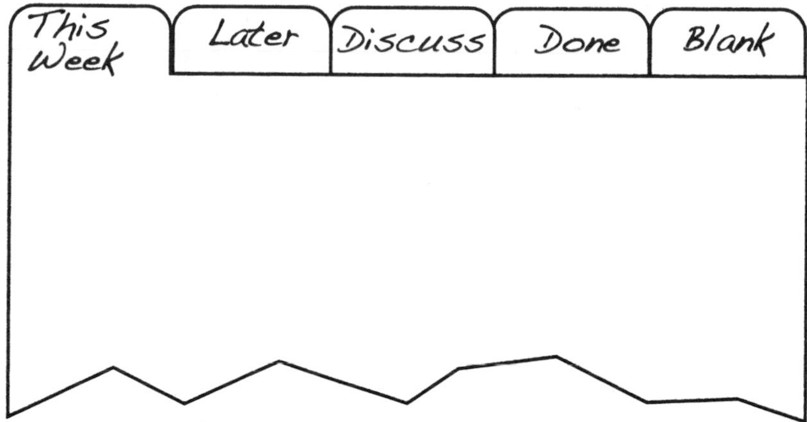

1. Every time you think of a task that needs to be completed, create a card for it and put that card in the "Discuss" section.

2. Schedule a regular meeting once or twice a week to sit down together and discuss the cards. Decide which tasks are the most important and can be reasonably done this week and hold on to them. Put the other cards, in basic order of importance, into the "Later" section.

3. The cards you are holding are the "This Week" tasks. Discuss what each task entails. Does "Finish the bathroom remodel" include painting, or just installing the toilet and laying tile? Who, exactly, will do the work? When, exactly, will it most likely get done? Do you have all the supplies? Do you both understand what the job entails? How many hours do you think it will take? Does any of it need to be hired out? Ask yourselves whether the number of tasks for this week seems reasonable once you know all the details. If you have too many tasks for the time you have available, take the least important and add them to the front of the "Later" section.

4. Put the remaining cards into "This Week" along with any notes you've added from your discussion that might be useful reminders (i.e. "tile and toilet only").

Go to the box each time you're ready to "tackle tasks" and work on something in the "This Week" section, preferably the first card. When a task is completed, put the card in the "Done" section.

This system can also be done electronically in a shared document, app, or bullet journal format.

Why This Works

This system works for a whole variety of reasons:

- Each week, the outstanding tasks are "re-prioritized." There are always more tasks to be done than can be completed; this helps ensure the most important are tackled first and that both partners agree on which are the top tasks.
- Both partners gain a more complete understanding of what the other partner contributes.
- The ADHD spouse benefits from the planning expertise of the non-ADHD spouse. While reviewing when and how a task is to be done, both members of the couple can assess whether the planning is realistic. In addition, the non-ADHD partner gains a better understanding of what the ADHD partner is thinking about the project; communication is clarified.
- The box, bullet journal, document or app is easy to locate, and progress can be tracked.
- This system relieves anxiety for the non-ADHD spouse. Every time she thinks of a task she can just write it down and be assured that it will get adequately discussed that week. Putting the task into the system means it will no longer be "hanging over her head." The benefits of this to both members of the couple are enormous.
- It helps the ADHD spouse remember which task to focus on (the first card in the box) thus helping ensure that a task gets finished completely before the next is started.

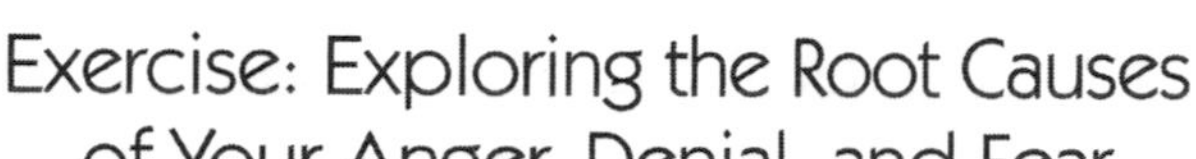

Exercise: Exploring the Root Causes of Your Anger, Denial, and Fear

This exercise provides a way to explore issues underlying your most difficult emotions so that you can talk about them more productively with your spouse. Either spouse can do it.

As one example, take a blank piece of paper and place it in a landscape (horizontal) direction. Pick a topic you are angry about, and write it in brief in the middle of the paper. This is your "main issue." Then start brainstorming about the elements of that topic that make you angry. Position them around the main issue, like satellites. If you have two items that are related, put them near each other. Keep asking yourself "what else?" until you feel you've gotten all your ideas onto the page. Once you've written down these "satellite" ideas, go to one satellite and ask yourself, "Why does this bother me? What's underneath my anger?" Write the answer near the satellite. Pursue this web of ideas until you feel you've gotten all of your thoughts about the main and satellite ideas on paper. Then "prune" and "connect" ideas. Link those that are related by lines. Cross off those that aren't as important, now that you reflect them. Highlight emotional ideas or themes that have emerged. It will look messy, but that's okay; this is just an idea generator to get you thinking more deeply.

Examples are on the next pages. The main issue is "My husband doesn't do ANY chores!" The first chart is the main idea and satellites. The second adds the answers to "What's underneath my anger?"

Step 1 – Main Issue and Satellites

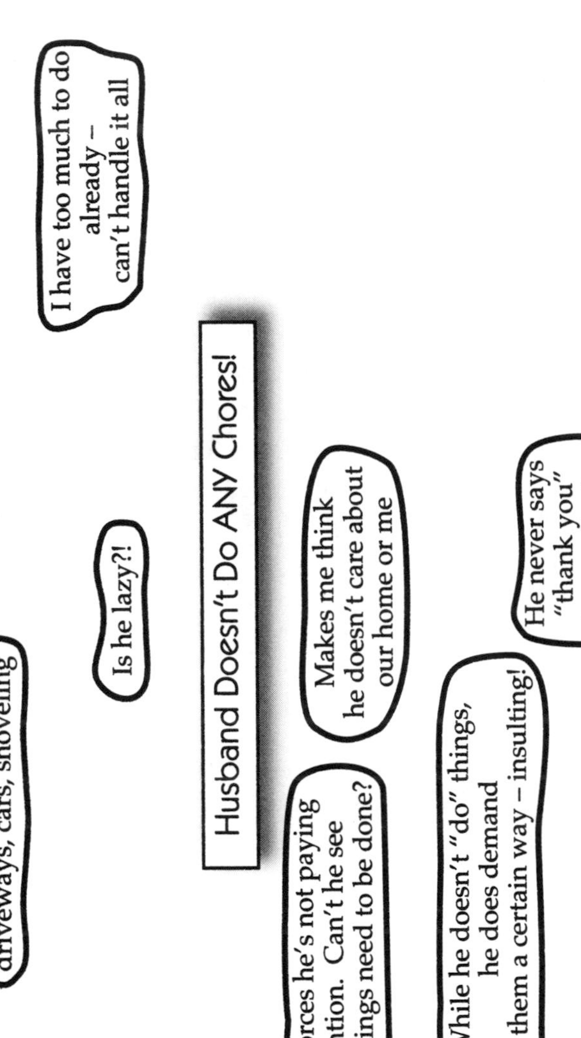

Step 2 – What's Underneath?

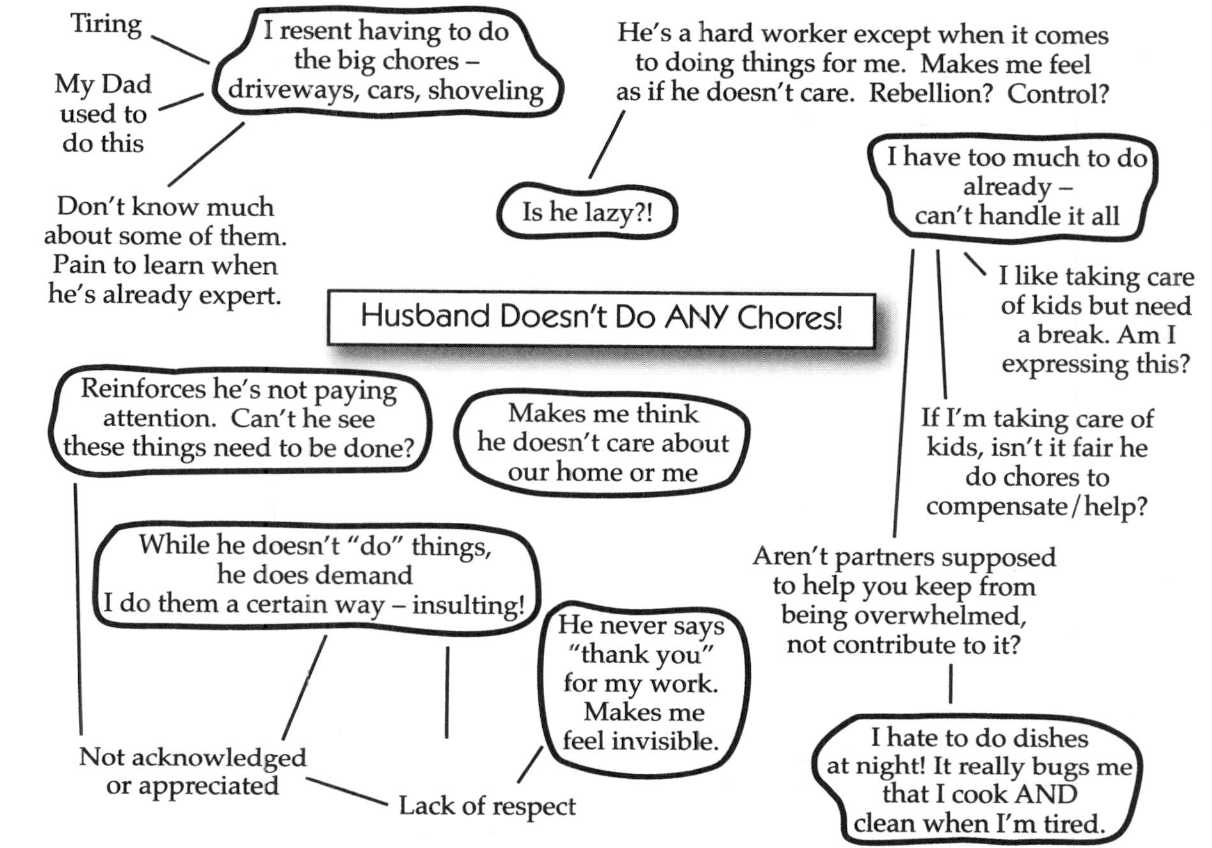

From this brainstorming you can see that there are some core emotional issues underneath the disagreement over chores:

- *Appreciation* – "not acknowledged or appreciated" and "he never says thank you"
- *Status* – "lack of respect"
- *Autonomy* – "while he doesn't 'do' things, he does demand I do them a certain way – insulting!"

Note that just because the husband's actions *communicate* to his spouse that he doesn't care, it doesn't mean that this is true. In relationships affected by ADHD symptoms, sometimes it's the symptoms doing the communicating, not the spouse. It's quite possible he doesn't understand that his actions communicate these ideas. So the next step here might include discussing the underlying issues in a calm way (try a learning conversation), and deciding what course of action you (the non-ADHD spouse) wish to take in response. Some possible actions include requesting calmly, but firmly, that your spouse start by taking on one meaningful chore for its symbolic meaning; hiring a cleaning service; and finding other ways for the spouse to clarify and communicate respect, appreciation, and caring. Continuing without addressing the underlying concerns about respect and love is not a good option.

Two-Day Validation Tracking Worksheet

For two days, note and rate every response you have toward each other. To do this well, you'll need to sit down about once an hour and think about your interactions during that hour. A "1" is a wonderful interaction that validated you or your partner; a "5" is an interaction that completely invalidated one of you. Any time you have an interaction, good or bad, write it down. Track your own behavior as well as your spouse's. This goes both ways.

Any of the following earn an automatic 5:

- Criticism
- Contempt
- Stonewalling
- Sarcasm
- Defensiveness
- Criticism masked as "help"

Paying no attention (for whatever reason) should also be noted in the poorer end of the spectrum (you can figure out later if it was due to the ADHD symptom of distraction or an intentional putdown).

At the end of the experiment, find some time to sit down together and talk about what you've discovered. There may be patterns, such as a non-ADHD spouse being particularly critical around the subject of not getting enough attention, in which case it's likely that many of the invalidating actions are centered around ADHD symptom responses. There may be areas of strength that you need to note, as well.

My hope is that this exercise will do three things for you:

1. Make you more aware of the frequency of destructive, invalidating behavior so you can diminish its presence in your lives.
2. Get you thinking about better, more validating, ways to respond in these same situations in the future.
3. Help you decide to reinforce existing validating interactions

You may find this exercise a bit depressing. But the first step in changing behaviors is identifying them.

Resources

Resources change continuously. For the most current information, visit ADHDmarriage.com

ADHD

The Couple's Guide to Thriving with ADHD
Melissa Orlov and Nancie Kohlenberger, LMFT (2014)

An award-winning extension of *The ADHD Effect on Marriage,* this book focuses in-depth upon emotional hot spots that couples impacted by ADHD have difficulty overcoming, even as they improve their relationship in general. It goes in-depth into those issues that are the greatest stumbling blocks, including anger, balancing responsibilities, gaining equal status, communication obstacles and improving intimacy and trust.

Delivered from Distraction
Edward M. Hallowell, MD, and John J. Ratey, MD (2005)

This book provides an excellent overview of what ADHD is all about and how you can get the most out of life with ADHD. The authors use a "strengths-based" approach to dealing with ADHD and view it as "a way of being" rather than a "disorder." They provide concrete information about how to treat ADHD and the common issues that people with ADHD encounter. *Driven to Distraction,* written ten years earlier by the same authors, is also still relevant today.

Women with Attention Deficit Disorder
Sari Solden, MS, LMFT (Revised 2005)

Women with ADHD face special issues related to their gender and societal expectations that most men with ADHD don't face. They encounter challenges when it comes to asserting themselves effectively to deal with ADHD. Solden is a real expert in this topic. If the woman in your couple has ADHD, this can be a life-changing book.

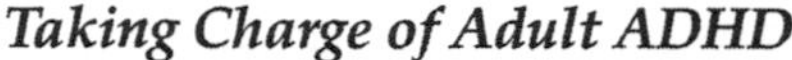

Taking Charge of Adult ADHD

Russell Barkley, Ph.D with Christine Benton (2010)

Diagrams, call outs and straight-forward prose help make this book on adult ADHD particularly appealing to adults with ADHD. Barkley is a top expert in the field, so the information is also scientifically sound.

More Attention, Less Deficit: Success Strategies for Adults with ADHD

Ari Tuckman, PsyD, MBA (2009)

This ADHD handbook is written in an even-toned, practical style and organized in brief articles that can be read in any sequence, letting the reader choose what to work on first. Though the book is long, it tackles issues in short, succinct articles, such as "Manage the Mail and Get the Bills Out on Time" and "Expectation Management: Promise Only What You Can Deliver" and "Is ADD an Excuse or an Explanation?" The book offers explanations for what is going on, as well as specific tactics for overcoming problems.

May We Have Your Attention Please?

Laura MacNioven, Med & J. Anne Bailey, Ph.D, CPsych

This fun workbook helps adults learn how to live with, and thrive with, ADHD. I think of is as a workbook for befriending your ADHD.

You Mean I'm Not Lazy, Stupid or Crazy?!

Kate Kelly and Peggy Ramundo (2006)

This book is extremely well organized, and provides many useful ideas for how to manage ADHD successfully. It is a good complement to *Delivered from Distraction* for those who are just starting to learn about ADHD, going into different aspects than *Delivered.* The sections on coping strategies and turning ideas into action are particularly good.

ADHD in Adults: What the Science Says
Russell A. Barkley, Kevin R. Murphy, and Mariellen Fischer (2008)

This 500-page book, filled with graphs and charts, is for those who want a look into some of the research about adult ADHD. The authors go into great detail about their ideas—spending 50 pages, for example, on why they believe ADHD in adults should be diagnosed differently than in children. Be prepared for lots of statistics, and many mentions of the word "disorder." This will tell you the unvarnished facts about ADHD. Written for very interested adults as well as researchers and practitioners.

Film & Video:

ADD & Loving It was first broadcast on Canadian TV. It's loads of fun, and informative as well.

How to ADHD is a well-produced, quick cut, and entertaining video series about ADHD that will particularly appeal to those with ADHD.

Websites:

The following websites are just some that contain helpful information about ADHD and support for adult ADHD:

adhdmarriage.com My website is the most complete platform for information about how ADHD impacts relationships.. Begin with "Start Here" and "Melissa's Favorite Posts" in the blog area. You can: contact me through the site; find reliable research; join a forum; download information about ADHD treatment; find support services such as my couples seminar, consulting and support groups, and much more.

adultadhdbook.com Ari Tuckman's site includes informative short videos about many aspects of ADHD.

ADDitudemag.com *ADDitude Magazine's* website includes lots of useful articles and resources. Use for inspiration rather than scientific accuracy.

caddac.ca The Centre for ADD / ADHD Advocacy in Canada hosts a complete list of resources and information for those living in Canada.

drhallowell.com Dr. Hallowell's site provides his inspiration, ideas and opinions about ADHD.

impactADHD.com Provides coaching for families impacted by ADHD who are trying to better support complex (often ADHD) kids.

CHADD.org One way to find a local support group, as well as background information.

Coping Skills

The Dance of Anger: A Woman's Guide to Changing the Patterns of Intimate Relationships
Harriet Lerner, PhD (2005)

If you or your spouse is experiencing any anger in your relationship and you can read only one more book, this is the one to pick. In my opinion, this bestseller is *the* best book on how to address anger, period.

Letting Go of Anger: The Eleven Most Common Anger Styles & What to Do About Them
Ronald Potter-Efron, MSW, Ph.D & Patricia Potter-Efron, MS

Take the quiz to identify your own anger styles, then learn how these styles help and hurts you, plus ways to improve your interactions.

ADD-Friendly Ways to Organize Your Life
Judith Kolberg & Kathleen Nadeau, Ph.D (2002)

Organized by problem area, this is the best book about strategies needed to become more organized and reliable if you have ADHD. A sampling of their topics: Learning to Prioritize; Chaos; Time Awareness; ADHD-Friendly Organizing.

The Mindfulness Prescription for Adult ADHD
Lidia Zylowska. MD (2012)

Mindfulness is a powerful way to improve attention, manage emotions and reach one's goals more effectively. This ADHD-oriented approach includes as CD of guided exercises.

Dare to Forgive
Edward M. Hallowell, MD (2004)

This gem of a book not only makes the case that the ability to forgive is a sign of strength, but it also provides a step-by-step process for moving from anger and distress to forgiveness. It is a very useful book for those who are caught up in a destructive cycle of anger and retaliation in their relationships.

Codependent No More: How to Stop Controlling Others and Start Caring For Yourself
Melody Beattie (1992)

This is the classic on codependency, and is a great help to those trying to step away from parent-child dynamics.

Communication Strategies

Beyond Reason: Using Emotions as You Negotiate
Roger Fisher and Daniel Shapiro (2006)

Although this book was written with a business audience in mind, it provides an excellent simplification of some of the basics for understanding and creating better ways to communicate. It's highly relevant for couples struggling to communicate through the often difficult emotions stimulated by dealing with ADHD. I highly recommend it.

Getting Past No: Negotiating in Difficult Situations
William Ury (2007)

If you wish to delve further into negotiation strategies, William Ury is another great choice. This book, or his *The Power of a Positive No: How to Say No and Still Get to Yes* can provide more ideas.

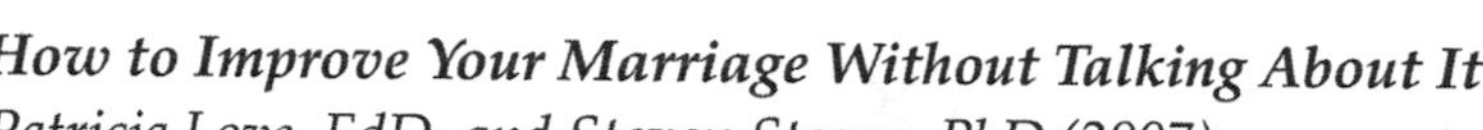

How to Improve Your Marriage Without Talking About It
Patricia Love, EdD, and Steven Stosny, PhD (2007)

One of the challenges of relationships isn't just ADHD, but also gender differences. This book explores two huge communication issues that couples experience: men's shame, and women's fears of loss and abandonment. These fears are heightened in ADHD relationships, as excessive shame is a common side effect of ADHD, and distraction on the part of a male partner with ADHD can lead his wife to feel abandoned.

Divorce, Separation, and Whether to Stay Married

Should I Stay or Go? How Controlled Separation (CS) Can Save Your Marriage
Lee Raffel, MSW (1999)

There is no doubt that many couples struggling with how ADHD affects their marriage contemplate divorce or separation, and many actually end up getting divorced. This book helps you to create your own answer to the basic question "Should I stay or go?" that desperate spouses may ask, and provides a number of ways to think through how a separation or divorce might proceed. Raffel is an advocate of "controlled separation" as a last-ditch effort to get some distance from each other and save a marriage, and she provides very specific guidelines for how couples might decide whether to try this route, as well as many examples and real-life stories.

Too Good to Leave, Too Bad to Stay: A Step-by-Step Guide to Help You Decide Whether to Stay In or Get Out of Your Relationship
Mira Kirshenbaum (1997)

This is an insightful and thoughtful guide to resolving relationship ambivalence (that period when you can't decide whether to stay in your marriage or leave it). Under the theory that relationships are too complicated to weigh good versus bad, Kirshenbaum offers 36 diagnostic tests against which you should measure your relationship and your feelings. She likens the process to how doctors diagnose illness. One caveat: be careful to look at whether unresolved anger around your relationship, or ADHD symptoms that can be treated and improved, unfairly biases your answers to the negative.

Index

K

L

M

N

O

P

Q

R

S